Harold Godwinson

The head of King Harold II on an rare silver penny struck during 1066.
PAS Unique ID: DENO-E3DCE5 Rights owner: Derby Museums Trust
Creative commons license:

Harold Godwinson

The life, death, mythology,
family, and legacy of
King Harold,
who died at Battle in 1066

Keith Foord

PER BELLUM PATRIA

ISBN 978-1-903099-11-7

First published in the UK by
Battle and District Historical Society
www.battlehistorysociety.com

Design and setting by Helm Information
amandahelm@uwclub.net
Cover design by Keith Foord

Printed by Ingram's Lightning Source
Lightning Source states that it expects its paper suppliers to be environmentally responsible,
and not use papers sourced from endangered old growth forests, forests of exceptional
conservation value, or the Amazon Basin.

Contents

The White Wyvern

A mythical creature, the wyvern is a two-legged, winged dragon, with a curved tail, that appeared as a white dragon on King Harold II Godwinson's gonfalon at the Battle of Hastings. It is a popular animal in European literature. The wyvern in its various forms and colours is an heraldic beast, appearing as a charge, supporter or crest on coats of arms, on flags etc. It is popular as a mascot for schools, sports teams, and military units especially in Wales and the Wessex area, but it is used across Europe and North America as a symbol of strength and endurance. It has a subliminal message that the wyvern is watching, keeping everything under control.

All the records suggest that Harold had strength, endurance, control, with 'no fault of rashness or levity', apart, some would say, his rash rush to confront William. The wyvern would have been a suitable symbolic representation for him. The white dragon was a symbol of Anglo-Saxon England, their mythical symbolic white dragon having gradually forced the equally mythical emblematic red dragon of the early Britons into the fastnesses of Wales, after the ingress of Germanic Saxon tribes into southern Britain after about 450CE.[1,2]

In the Bayeux Tapestry pairs of fire belching wyverns are seen three times in the lower border – under the scene where Harold is handed over from Guy of Ponthieu to William, just after the intriguing Ælfgyva scene, and as Norman horses are landed at Pevensey – maybe markers of times of perceived anxiety, stress or displeasure for Harold/England. Other wyverns without fiery breath, appear in the upper border – on the approach to Mont St Michel, where their tails are protectively wrapped around their bodies, and later on Harold's approach to Bayeux before the fateful oath, where their necks are stretched out and wings spread as if in alarm or warning. The wyvern gonfalon is seen in Harold's death scene, once flying bravely, and after both the standard bearer and Harold had fallen, trampled into the bloody ground.

1. As told in 'The Prophecies of Merlin' in Geoffrey of Monmouth's *History of the Kings of Britain* as an allegory for the cultural displacement of British tribes into Wales by the Anglo-Saxons.

2 There is undoubtedly confusion about two and four legged dragons in mythology. Certainly, the four-legged dragon now appears on the flag of Wales, although some early histories describe the Welsh dragon as two legged, and before the 16th century both bi- and quadra-pedal dragons were just called 'dragons'. The two-legged winged wyvern 'dragon' is used here due to its prominence in the Bayeux Tapestry.

Wyvern images on this page, the covers and throughout the book ©BDHS

List of Figures

Abbreviations commonly used in the text

ASC(X) *Anglo-Saxon Chronicle* [version letter(s) in brackets]
BT   *The Bayeux Tapestry*
BDHS   Battle and District Historical Society
Carmen *The Carmen de Hastingae Proelio*
CBA   *Chronicle of Battle Abbey*
CWA   *Chronicle of Waltham Abbey*
Domesday *Domesday Book,*
'by Domesday' = 'by 1086'
John of Worcester   John of Worcester's *Chronicon ex Chronicis*
PASE   The Prosopography of Anglo-Saxon England website
PASE Domesday   The Domesday section in the PASE website
OF, OE, ON, L   Old French, Old English, Old Norse, Latin

Significant Website Acknowledgements

The following websites have been accessed many times during the writing of this book (between August 2020 and October 2021)

https://www.bayeuxmuseum.com/la-tapisserie-de-bayeux/
decouvrir-la-tapisserie-de-bayeux/explorer-la-tapisserie-de-
bayeux-en-ligne/
https://epns.nottingham.ac.uk/
https://domesday.pase.ac.uk/
https://opendomesday.org/
https://pase.ac.uk/jsp/index.jsp

Foreword

What do we know about Harold Godwinson, briefly king of the English in 1066? And 'was it all Harold's fault'? Keith Foord's latest contribution to the publications of the Battle and District Historical Society brings together a lot of the evidence for Harold's life and does justice to modern scholarship.

Beginning with the rise of his father Godwin, the book provides a vivid and thought provoking narrative. It inevitably devotes a lot of attention to the dramatic period from 1051 to 1066 and to the many controversies that surround the interpretation of those years, but it also supplies context. All readers will find the many translations from primary sources an invaluable aid to reaching their own conclusions.

The local knowledge of members of the Society is splendidly deployed to bring alive the events that followed Duke William's landing at Pevensey. The final chapter on Harold's family after his death contains much rich material.

The Appendix 'It's all Harold's fault', a title paraphrased above, goes beyond historiography to show how alive Harold's legacy is today, a point that is also made with many superb illustrations.

Professor David Bates
President, Battle and District Historical Society

Introduction

An interpretive synopsis can be found here looking into the life and death of Harold Godwinson, with the many ambivalences as well as missed possibilities which occur in his life, and in stories of his death and their consequences for his family and for England.

It does not take much reading around to quickly realise that English historical outcomes could have been quite different in 1066. Conventional history has its limitations and cannot explain exactly what happened when Harold met William in Normandy in either 1064 or 1065 and even exactly why Harold was there. The consequences of that fateful visit could have been quite dissimilar from those described by the early post-Conquest writers, and by those writing years after the event. Nor is his death and the fate of his body spared ambiguity. And how did his surviving family fare?

This book was inspired by being asked to give a talk on theories surrounding the Battle of Hastings and the death of King Harold Godwinson. Discussions about the life and death of Harold with Professor David Bates have also made me seek out the most recent pre-Conquest histories, of which David Bates's own most recent biography of William the Conqueror and Tom Licence's of Edward the Confessor are exemplars. They look deeply into and query historical events in a very critical way, significantly different from the approaches of only fifty years ago.

Reading the above and other secondary sources, as well as primary sources, we can soon imagine that what we are told in the oldest stories was the distorted news of the day, written with more than an eye on what was safe to write about, what had happened, who the actors involved were and their rank and rationality. Sounds familiar? This is still happening today; it could be partial or total fake news. The 'Harold story' has been further distorted by the literary noise of nearly a millennium, romantic tales in old sagas and modern fiction, and other media and political spins in various earlier eras, not just our own.

We all hear what we want to hear. Standing back and trying to separate fact from fiction is virtually impossible. Freud knew this and knew that people made things up to fit the reality they wished for. This gives rise to multiple explanations of what actually occurred, which we can only sift for probability.

You may think this comment odd – but the interpretations of Harold's life and death which are probably the most acceptable are the historically conventional ones. Many great minds have argued over the facts and interpretations, sometimes very fiercely indeed, and far be it that a humble local historian should reinterpret things, so here, for example, the conventional battle site is assumed. That does not mean that credible alternatives cannot be considered, historians should always have an open mind.

To keep the story as straightforward as possible in this book, it is also assumed that the Norman landing areas and battle sites are as described in BDHS's previous book, *1066 and the Battle of Hastings – Prologues, Events and Postscripts.* Harold turned up for a battle which led to his (almost certain) death. It does not matter to the historical outcome to know precisely where he finally fell: his actual death was the fulcrum for a huge political change in England. So, although suggestions of alternative battlefields for the Battle of Hastings are entirely reasonable to make, I have not ventured deeply into analyses of the options of other sites that have been suggested for this battle, nor of any other battles, as the location of sites does not influence the historical outcomes. It is fun to think laterally and ask questions, exploring alternatives which were possible. But a burden of reasonable proof, accuracy, probability and probity exists on those who propound ideas, taking into account all the records which exist and their sources, historical geography and medieval battle strategies. Also, where doubts exist in the story of Harold's life they should be expressed, but again analysed for probability, which is all we can do with these nearly 1000-year-old accounts – or more uncertainty than already exists will overwhelm, distract from and distort the whole.

There is some reuse of words from both *BC to 1066* and *1066 and the Battle of Hastings*. Both books had different foci, although covering the timescale of Harold's life, so this is not surprising, and each book stands alone. Here the focus is on one man, Harold Godwinson, and the work is deepened and expanded considerably to concentrate on his life, family and motivations.

How have the British viewed Harold's defeat and the Norman Conquest over the years since 1066? Inspired after reading Majorie Chibnall's *The Debate on the Norman Conquest* and David Douglas's 1946 lecture *The Norman Conquest and British Historians*, which is a superb synopsis of historical thinking up to the mid-20th century about how historians had moved with the political tides, I realised that interpretations of the long-term effects Harold's death and the Norman Conquest, since the immediate post-Conquest period until the beginning of the 21st century, have varied very significantly over the centuries. These interpretations were influenced by the concurrent dynastic regimes, geo-politics, economics, social criteria and visions. Seldom was any great rigour or critical questioning attached to these varied constructs until towards the end of the 19th century, and indeed sometimes it could be personally dangerous for historians to try to use such tools. It is chastening to realise that history could not be regarded as a dispassionate science until the dawn of the 20th century and even now there are disagreements. So in Part 2, I ask if this was all Harold's fault and give an overview of how perceptions of this event have changed down the centuries.

I hope that you find the content of the book fascinating. If, after this, you want to read more about the battle and the multiple events which led up to it, please see the book that I wrote with my colleague, Neil Clephane-Cameron, *1066 and the Battle of Hastings – Preludes, Events and Postscripts.* Some of Neil's words from that book will be found scattered through this volume for which I thank him. The advice that Professor John Gillingham, a past President of BDHS, kindly gave when writing that book still shows through here. I also particularly thank both Professor David Bates, present President of BDHS, for discussions and his willing, gentle criticisms and expert guidance particularly pointing me to numbers of less well known facts and sources, and Mme Sylvette Lemagnen, retired Curator of the *Bayeux Tapestry*, who is a present Vice President of BDHS, for her kind advice and comments on all matters concerning French spellings and the Tapestry. Other members of BDHS proof read and criticised drafts, so thanks are also due particularly to Neil Clephane-Cameron, for his medieval and classical military knowledge and for pointing out the differences between red and white wyverns, Alan Judd for a style review, tips and encouragement, George Kiloh, BDHS' guru of punctuation and for local research, Hugh Willing for his military strategy advice, Gina Doherty for local research and a double check on the descent line of Harold Godwinson to the present Royal family, and Amanda Helm for her book design and setting skills, as well for her incisive criticism of my first concept paper, which sent me back to the drawing board and much improved this book.

Tina Greene gave permission to use an image from her *Battle Tapestry*, Chas Jones kindly sent the image of the Fulford Tapestry, Heather Cawte arranged to send recent images of sections of the recently finalised Stamford Bridge Tapestry, and Fanny Garbe, chargée de communication et promotion at the Bayeux Museum, and Erin O'Shea of the BBC News Permissions Team are thanked for granting permission to use images from the Bayeux Tapestry. And of course, my wife Paula must be thanked for those many cups of tea, coffee, biscuits, an occasional cake, and a critical read through of early drafts.

A selected bibliography is provided of the sources, some quite obscure, that I have used at some point in preparation. Many others have puzzled their way via this route, and many have said much the same things in different ways. Perhaps needless to say, any opinions expressed in this book are mine unless ascribed elsewhere. Any errors or misinterpretations remain mine, as a synopsis can never be perfect. Quotes and images used are acknowledged where possible. If by chance I have missed any that should have been acknowledged or infringed any copyrights, apologies. BDHS will do its best to remedy matters in any subsequent edition.

BDHS is a registered charity with the objective of educating the public in history related to Battle and the surrounding area of eastern Sussex. This includes investigation, discussion and publication of all matters relating to that objective. Any surplus from any BDHS publication is reinvested, and no officer, member or author of a BDHS publication receives any financial reward, excepting genuine expenses. BDHS as a publisher is a non-commercial entity, as BDHS policy is that its publications overall should not result in a surplus. Fortunately, as a few books sell well, this gives it much flexibility to publish on some less well-known subjects and aspects of local history, which otherwise could only be printed and sold at a loss.

We are of course privileged that a major event of history happened here at Battle in 1066. The death of Harold was truly 'big bang' local history with national, European and eventually worldwide consequences. Some of my ancestors lived in the area in the 16th century, and probably before that; if they were in the area in September and October 1066 they would have been terrified. I was born in Hastings and live in Battle. Hastings, Battle, and the surrounding eastern Sussex region are honoured historical places in which to have roots.

Keith Foord,
Battle
November 2021

Godwifu? (Godiva)

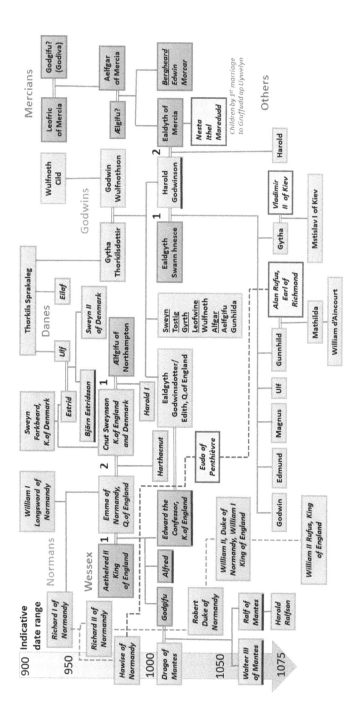

Fig. 1. The main cast: Family relationships and major English, Danish, Norman, Breton and other connections of Harold Godwinson. ©BDHS

The past is uncertain. This may lead to an uncoupling of our historical understandings from their loose anchors in imagined accuracy.

Timeline 984–1100

It is often not possible to assign events to specific years in this era, so it should be recognised that some dates are (very) approximate.

Within each year multiple events are ordered in time sequence, if known.

Year	Event
984	Birth of Emma of Normandy
994	Massive Viking attacks on London involving Sweyn Forkbeard
997	Gytha Thorkelsdóttir, future wife of Earl Godwin Wulfnothson born
1001	Godwin Wulfnothson born
1002	Emma of Normandy marries King Aethelred II
1003x1005	Birth of Edward the Confessor
1009	Thurkill the Tall arrives in East Anglia
1012	King Aethelred II pays Sweyn of Denmark 48,000 pounds of silver as Danegeld
1013	King Sweyn of Denmark invades England, via the Humber and River Trent. Aethelred II takes Emma, Edward, Alfred and Godgifu to Normandy. Sweyn of Denmark briefly takes the throne of England by conquest, but dies soon afterwards.
1014	Sweyn of Denmark dies in February. Wulfnoth Cild, father of Earl Godwin died about now. Aethelred II returns. Sweyn's son Cnut returns to Denmark
1015	Thurkill reunites with Cnut. Cnut Sweynson invades England in the summer via Poole Harbour and the River Frome. Cnut accepts submission of Wessex.
1016	Cnut ravages Warwickshire. Cnut ravages Northumbria goes south to London. English turncoat Eadric Streona's lands in west Midlands ravaged. Cnut accepted by Londoners.

1016	Earl Uhtred of Northumbria submits to Cnut but is murdered on Cnut's order. Battles of Penselwood and Sherston are both stalemates. Battle of Brentford – Edmund Ironside wins. 2nd Battle of Otford – Edmund Ironside wins. Battle of Assunden – Cnut wins. Accord of Ola's Isle – Cnut and Edmund share England. Edmund Ironside dies, maybe assassinated – Cnut now King of all England. Execution of many untrusted English nobles
1017	Cnut divides England into Earldoms of Wessex, Mercia, East Anglia and Northumbria. Edmund Ironside's children sent to Sweden, moved on to Kiev. Erik of Hlàthir appointed Earl of Northumbria, Thurkill Earl of East Anglia. Queen Emma flees to Normandy with children Edward, Alfred and Godgifu. Cnut marries Emma of Normandy, widow of Aethelred II. Eadric Streona, Earl of Mercia, executed
1018	Godwin Wulfnothson becomes Earl of eastern Wessex
1019	War in Denmark. Cnut rewards Godwin with a wife, Gytha
1020	Aethelnoth, probable relative of Godwin, made Archbishop of Canterbury. Godwin is now Earl of all Wessex, except Kent. Sweyn Godwinson born.
1021	Cnut outlaws Thurkill.
1022	Harold Godwinson's presumed year of birth.
1023	Reconciliation of Cnut and Thurkill, who is regent in Denmark.
1025	Edith Godwinsdotter born.
1026	Thurkill disappears, replaced by Ulf, brother of Godwin's wife Gytha. Tostig Godwinson born. In Normandy Richard II dies, Richard III inherits.
1027	Richard III dies, Robert (to be father of William), inherits.
1028	Cnut deposes Olaf II as King of Norway.
1030	Cnut offers widowed sister Estrid to Duke Robert of Normandy. Gyrth Godwinson born.
1034	Olaf's son Magnus gains throne of Norway from the regent, Sweyn, son of Cnut.

1035	Cnut dies, son Harthacnut now King in Denmark. Sharing of England between Harold Harefoot and Harthacnut, latter represented by Queen Emma. Robert I, Duke of Normandy dies. William made Duke of Normandy.
1032x1037	Aelfgifu Godwinsdotter born Gunnhilda Godwinsdotter born Leofwine Godwinson born *(these 3 births must be spread out)*
1036	Attempt by Edward to invade England at Southampton repulsed. Alfred's attempt to visit Emma ambushed at Guildford, he was blinded and died at Ely.
1037	Harefoot now protector of all England
1038	Godwin adds Kent to Wessex, now controls all of English Channel coast. Approximate birth date of Alfgar Godwinson, believed to have become a monk at Reims, if he ever existed
1039	Gruffydd Ap Llewellyn becomes King of Gwynedd and Powys, starts making trouble on English/Welsh borders, to last until 1062
1040	Harefoot dies, Harthacnut becomes King. Wulfnoth Godwinson born
1040x1042	Emma commissions the start of the *Encomium Emma Reginae*
1041	Edward invited to join half-brother Harthacnut and Emma in England.
1042	Harthacnut dies. Edward becomes King. Magnus takes Denmark
1043	Edward crowned. Edward deprived his mother Emma of her lands and wealth.
1044	Harold Earl of East Anglia. Edith Swan-neck becomes Harold's concubine.
1045	King Edward marries Edith Godwinsdotter, sister of Harold
1046	Earl Sweyn Godwinson abducts the Abbess of Leominster
1047	Earl Sweyn exiled. Harold blockades channel to Baldwyn V of Flanders at request of Emperor Henry III. Harold may stop Abbey of Fécamp taking possession of manor of Steyning. Possible birth of Hákon Sweynson
1048	Raids into Essex, Harold's navy sees them off

1049	Sweyn Godwinson returns, murders cousin Bjorn. Declared *nithing*. Council of Reims
1050	Possible date of last revision/addition to the *Encomium of Queen Emma*
1051	Edward appoints Robert Champart as Archbishop of Canterbury. Godwin and his sons revolt, declared outlaws. William Duke of Normandy reported to visit King Edward. Odda appointed Earl of western Wessex. Tostig Godwinson marries Judith of Flanders
1052	Godwin and family restored. Robert Champart flees, he might have taken Hákon Sweynson and Wulfnoth Godwinson as hostages to Robert of Normandy. Queen Emma dies. Sweyn Godwinson dies whilst returning from his penitential pilgrimage to the Holy Land
1053	Godwin Wulfnothson, Earl of Wessex dies. Harold Godwinson appointed Earl of Wessex and 'Dux Anglorum'. Aelfgar becomes Earl of East Anglia Duke William makes a controversial marriage with Mathilda of Flanders
1054	Battle of Mortemer, Guy of Ponthieu captured. Sent to William who imprisons him.
1055	Tostig Godwinson appointed Earl of Northumbria after Earl Siward's death. Earl Aelfgar outlawed. Gunnhild Haroldsdotter born. Aelfgar restored
1056	Earl Odda dies, western Wessex rejoined to the eastern part. Emperor Henry III dies. Harold visits Flanders. Agreement at Regensberg that Atheling Edward and his family should come to England
1056x1057	Harold visits Rome

1057	Atheling Edward arrives in England with his family from Hungary. Atheling Edward dies, children including Edgar placed in Royal household. Earl Leofric of Mercia dies, earldom passes to Aelfgar. Earldom of East Anglia, vacated by Aelfgar goes to Gyrth Godwinson. New Earldom covering area from Buckinghamshire to Kent created, goes to Leofwine Godwinson. Earl Aelfgar allies with Gruffydd Ap Llewellyn, he was banished. Gruffydd Ap Llewellyn married Ealdgyth of Mercia. Birth of Nest(a) ferch Gruffydd
1060	Harold has rebuilt the church at Waltham Death of King Henri I of France
1061	Tostig and Gyrth visit Rome. Scots invade Cumbria.
1062	Earl Aelfgar dies, son Edwin inherits Mercia. Possible oath by magnates to support Atheling Edgar as successor to Edward the Confessor. Harold and Tostig cause Gruffydd Ap Llewellyn to flee Death of Pope Nicholas II, Pope Alexander II elected
1063	Welsh attack Herefordshire
1064	Gruffydd Ap Llewellyn assassinated
1064x1065	Harold's Fishing trip. Harold in Normandy
1065	Harold returns to England with Hákon Sweynsson. Northumbria revolts against Tostig, Harold investigates. Tostig deprived of Earldom of Northumbria, goes to Flanders. Morcar becomes Earl of Northumbria. Ælfgifu Godwinsdotter probably becomes Abbess of Wilton Abbey. Osulf II/Oswulf appointed Morcar's deputy north of the Tyne (Bernicia). Harold, Edwin and Morcar divide Tostig's Northumbrian manors between them Consecration of Westminster Abbey

1066	Edward the Confessor dies. Harold crowned King of England. Harold marries Ealdgyth of Mercia, Edwin and Morcar's sister, widow of Gruffydd. Halley's comet appears (April 24 – until mid-July) Tostig raids south and east coasts, beaten off in east by Morcar and Edwin Harold holds army and fleet ready around the Solent. English army stood down for harvest, fleet returns to London. Hardrada and Tostig raid north-east coast. Hardrada and Tostig enter Humber and sail up the River Ouse to Riccall. Battle of Fulford Gate, Edwin and Morcar lose. York surrenders to Hardrada and Tostig. Battle of Stamford Bridge, Harold wins, Hardrada and Tostig killed. Harold visits Waltham en route south Harold back in London. Battle of Hastings: Harold and brothers Gyrth and Leofwine die. Winchester falls to William; Queen Edith submits and aligns with William. Wilton mint ceases production of Harold II coins. Atheling Edgar promoted to be king but support not strong enough. Surrender at Berkhamsted by Archbishop Ealdred, Atheling Edgar, Earls Edwin and Morcar, other bishops and 'all the best men from London' (ASC(D) and John of Worcester) William crowned King of England at Christmas
1067	Ælfgifu Godwinsdotter, probably Abbess of Wilton, dies. Birth of Harold Haroldson to Ealdgyth of Mercia. Godwin and Edmund (possibly with Magnus) go to Ireland. Battle of Mechain: death of stepsons of Harold's wife, Edith of Mercia – Ithel/Idwal ap Gruffydd at the battle, and Maredudd ap Gruffydd soon afterwards.
1068	Siege of Exeter, probably in January maybe into February. Godwin and Edmund Haroldson attack Bristol and raid in Somerset. Gytha Thorkelsdóttir and daughter Gunnhild Godwinsdotter flee to Denmark from Exeter via Flatholm Island in the Bristol Channel. Chew Valley silver penny coin hoard probably buried.
1069	Godwin and Edmund Haroldson raid in Devon. Ralf de Gaël, a Breton, given most of the lands of Edith Swan-neck. He was also made Earl of Norfolk about now. He had been a leading Breton at the Battle of Hastings

1070	Gytha Thorkelsdóttir, wife of Earl Godwin dies. Ealdgyth of Mercia and son Harold Haraldsson flee to Ireland. Approximate date of marriage of Nest(a) ferch Gruffydd, Harold's stepdaughter, to Osbern fitzRichard son of Richard fitzScrob of Richards Castle
1072x1073	Gunnhilda Haroldsdotter leaves Winton convent and partners with Count Alan Rufus, Earl of Richmond, a kinsman of William I, about now. They have a child, probably named Mathilda, a year or so later
1075	Gytha Haroldsdotter marries Vladimir II Monomakh. Edith Godwinsdotter, Queen Edith, dies after a long illness, possibly leprosy, and is buried in Westminster Abbey. Ralf de Gaël rebels in Brittany against William. His English manors (previously of Edith Swan-neck) are forfeited and passed to Count Alan Rufus
1087	Gunnhild Godwinsdotter dies at Bruges. King William I dies in September. Wulfnoth Godwinson, Ulf Godwinson released. Ulf Haroldson last heard of. William's second son William II Rufus crowned King of England. His oldest son Robert Curthose becomes Duke Robert II of Normandy.
1089	About now Mathilda, daughter of Gunnhilda Godwinsdotter and Alan Rufus, marries Walter d'Aincourt. They have two sons, one called William. William d'Aincourt[1] sometime later (?after 1092x1100) dies in wardship at the court of William II Rufus. Mathilda gives land (formerly of Alan Rufus') plus gifts to Lincoln Cathedral and St Marys Abbey, York
1093	Alan Rufus, Earl of Richmond dies. Gunnhild seeks his brother Alan Niger's protection. Gunnhild exchanges letters and meets with Archbishop Anselm of Canterbury.
1094	Wulfnoth Godwinson dies at Salisbury
1097	Gunnhild Haroldsdotter dies.
1098	Harold Haroldson last heard of campaigning with Magnus III of Norway.
1100	King William II Rufus dies in a hunting accident in New Forest. Henry I becomes King of England

1 Also known as d'Eyncourt, d'Eincourt, Deincourt and Deyncourt

Godwin Wulfnothson, Harold Godwinson's father rose to power under King Cnut in 1018 and, through careful dealings, cunning and a willingness to switch sides, survived and served every king of England after that, until his death from natural causes in 1052.

1

The Rise of Godwin Wulfnothson, Harold's father

King Cnut (Knútr/Canute) made Godwin Wulfnothson, and thus his family, including his second son Harold Godwinson. The story of Harold would therefore not make sense without knowing how Cnut became King of England and how Harold's father who became Earl Godwin of Wessex, came to prominence. And on a wider scale why the Danish conquest of 1016 helped created the scenarios of 1066.

In the summer of 1015 the Danish prince, Cnut Sweynssen with a Danish army loaded into hundreds of longboats, invaded England by sea – penetrating its southern underbelly, via Poole Harbour and the River Frome, then thrusting northwards into the English midlands and further north to Northumbria.

This was with the support of his brother, King Harald II of Denmark, who had become king there after the death of their father King Sweyn. Sweyn himself had briefly conquered England in 1013, but then had died suddenly in early 1014. After that the English chased out his son Cnut, who cruelly mutilated his hostages before leaving. The English managed to regain control of their country, but it was but a brief interlude. Cnut came back the next year with serious intent.

Cnut's lieutenant was the powerful Thurkill Struthharaldsen 'the Tall' who was an elite mercenary.[1] Thurkill had first come to England in 1009 and had settled in East Anglia. He knew England well, as he and his 3,000 Jömviking mercenaries had been foolishly hired to help the defence of England by Cnut's predecessor, Æthelred II, King of England, against other Danes – particularly against Cnut's father, Sweyn of Denmark. In spite of Thurkill's 'protection', in 1012 Sweyn had received no less than 48,000 pounds of silver from the ill-advised Æthelred to stop raiding and go away, a huge Danegeld payment, and an immense burden on the English poor.

Thurkill defected back to Denmark to join Cnut in August 1015. Cnut's campaign in England is depicted on the map (figure 2) overleaf. He ravaged the south-west, receiving the submission of western Wessex, then marched northwards to lay waste Warwickshire, and further north to wreak havoc in Northumbria. In revenge the

English under Edmund Ironside, a son of Æthelred II by his first marriage to Ælfgifu,[2] and Ealdorman Uhtred of Northumbria, married to Æthelred's daughter, also named Ælfgifu, plundered the English turncoat Eadric Steona's lands in the west midlands. In March, Cnut slipped past Uhtred and took York. Uhtred then submitted to Cnut and agreed to meet him under safe conduct to formally submit at a place called Wiheal, probably near Tadcaster. The unarmed Uhtred and 40 of his men were savagely murdered at this meeting on Cnut's behalf by a man called Thurbrand and his men.[3] This was not the first sign of Cnut's ruthlessness and would not be the last.

Cnut went south again and gained London after a long siege, but then had to confront Ironside, first at Penselwood[4] in Somerset, on the Wiltshire/Dorset border, then Sherston in Wiltshire, both of which battles were stalemates. Cnut retreated to reinforce but was chased by Ironside. London was relieved followed shortly by the Battle of Brentford where the English had a victory sometime after May 1016, soon after Aethelred II's death on 23 April 1016, and then later at the 2nd Battle of Otford[5] in north Kent. Cnut retreated to the Isle of Sheppey and regrouped once more, later using his ships to cross the Thames estuary to Essex. The Danes raided into south Mercia until they were confronted by Ironside, whom they beat at the Battle of Assunden[6] on 18 October 1016.

Ironside retreated to Ola's Island [*ASC(F)*] in the River Severn near Deerherst[7], he was followed by Cnut who made a sharing accord with him there in late October. The main points of the campaign are shown as a map (figure 2). Edmund Ironside was to hold Wessex and Cnut the rest of England, although interestingly *John of Worcester* records 'that the crown of England remained with Edmund'. After a very brief period of dual kingship by Cnut and Ironside the latter conveniently died, maybe assassinated,[8] on 30th November 1016, when Cnut, following the agreement with Ironside which again according to *John of Worcester* was apparently endorsed by the magnates of England and putting aside Edmund's living brothers, became King of all England. The stress was on the magnates' acceptance of the wish of the dying king and tacit acceptance of the new king's lordship. Edmund was buried with his grandfather King Edgar at Glastonbury.

Ironside's children, including a son, Edward, were despatched by Cnut to Sweden to be 'disappeared', but somehow made their way first to Yaroslav of Kiev and then to the care of the King of Hungary, where they stayed and settled. Thus, a critical person in the stories is placed, for 'Edward the Exile' had a son Edgar with the wife he had married in Hungary, Agatha/Agafia – and Edgar was to have a significant rôle in the later pre and post 1066 stories.[9]

At the same time, Æthelred II's second wife, Emma, and her three children, Edward, Alfred and Godgifu, fled to safety in Normandy to the care of Emma's brother, Duke Richard II. This Edward was another critical person as in due course he would become King Edward the Confessor of England.

In early 1017 Cnut divided England into four parts, Wessex, Mercia, East Anglia

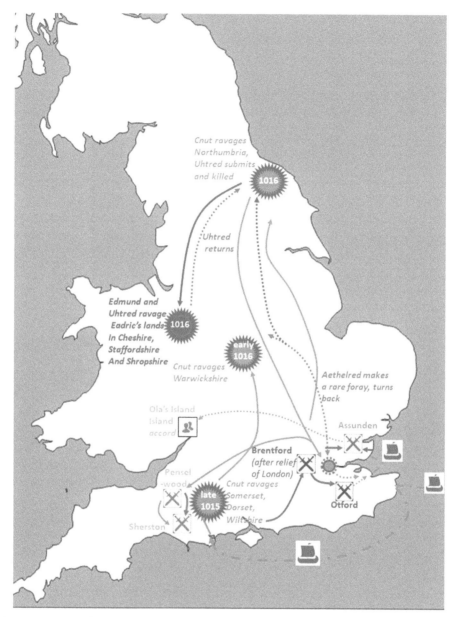

Fig. 2. Movements during Cnut's invasion and campaign (blue) and Edmund Ironside's defence of England (red). Inconclusive events in green. © BDHS

and Northumbria. He ruled Wessex directly but gave the Earldom of East Anglia to Thurkill. Northumbria went to Earl Eric Håkonssen of Lade[10] and Mercia to Eadric Streona. The duplicitous Eadric did not last long and was executed at Christmas 1017.

Cnut had won a country that was politically volatile but administratively had a surprisingly stable government. He went on to weigh the pros and cons of making a political marriage. He was already married 'in the Danish way' to Ælfgifu of Northampton, whom he was prepared to 'put aside'. William of Malmesbury offers the best explanation of the rationale behind the deal he then made to marry Æthelred II's widow, Emma – there would be some placation of the English and reconciliation with Normandy, and he would also hope to minimise any ambitious thoughts that Richard II of Normandy might have for his nephews Edward and Alfred to eventually seek their birthright. A deal was done. Cnut 'had her fetched' in 1017. Not long afterwards, probably about 1018 (but before 1023) Harthacnut (ON Hörthaknútr) was born.

Edward and Alfred prudently stayed in Normandy to be brought up in the ducal Norman household. Emma's last child by Cnut was a daughter, Gunnhild who was married at a young age to the future Emperor, Henry III of Germany in 1036.

In 1018 a further reorganisation saw Godwin Wulfnothson, a Sussex thane, and son of Wulfnoth Cild,[11] become Earl of Eastern Wessex. Godwin had campaigned against Cnut during the latter's invasion of England, but after that had fully supported him. Godwin fought by Cnut's side in Denmark, after Cnut's brother had died and Cnut had claimed the throne of Denmark, which he duly gained. Godwin had greatly impressed Cnut who said he was

the most cautious in counsel and the most active in war.

Cnut later 'gave' him his brother-in-law Ulf's sister Gytha Thorkelsdóttir as a wife, as well as eastern Wessex as an earldom. Thus, Earl Godwin Wulfnothson and his subsequent family came within Cnut's family circle, became related to the Danish royal family, and started to rise in importance.

In another move in 1020 Cnut made Æthelnoth, son of ealdorman Æthelmaer and a probable relative of Godwin, Archbishop of Canterbury.[12] Æthelnoth's appointment was possibly a gesture of appeasement and goodwill by the king towards Earl Godwin, as one of the earl's uncles, Æthelweard, had been executed by Cnut in his ruthless bloody cull of 1017, when he had disposed of many unreliable men and turncoats, including Eadric Steona, as above. He also outlawed Eadwig Atheling, the last remaining son of Aethelred II. Eadwig would later foolishly return and met a predictably sticky end.

The Anglo-Saxon Chronicle [*ASC(E)*] records that King Cnut outlawed Thurkill in November 1021, but later says that they entered a pact of reconciliation in 1023 [ASC(C)] under which Thurkill would act as regent in Denmark. As part of this deal they kept a son of each other's as hostage, which presumably meant that Cnut's son Harthacnut by his second queen, Emma, widow of Æthelred II, became a hostage to fortune. Thurkill remained regent in Denmark for about three more years, then unexplainedly disappears from the story, being replaced by Ulf Thorkelssen, Cnut's brother-in-law, married to his sister, Estrid Svendsdatter.

Ulf was also brother-in-law to Earl Godwin who was married to his sister Gytha

Thorkelsdóttir. Ulf died in 1026x27, probably killed on Cnut's order, but not before he had sired a son called Swein, who would in due course become King Swein II Estridssen, the first king of the House of Estridssen, 55 of which would rule Denmark from 1047 to 1375. To complicate family and diplomatic matters later, there is a garbled record that, in about 1030, Cnut offered his widowed sister Estrid/Margaret in marriage to Duke Robert of Normandy (William's father) who either refused her or rapidly divorced her saying that:

she was hateful to him.

Relationships between Normandy and Cnut's England deteriorated for a while after this.

Godwin was progressing rapidly and by 1020 was Earl of all Wessex, excluding Kent, after Ealdorman Æthelweard of the western provinces , a son of Æthelmær the Stout, was outlawed in 1020. The extended earldom would have been granted along with a significant number of manors, the income from which was designed to support the earl in the manner to which earls were accustomed and to support its administration, and defence. Down the years he accumulated yet more manors from grants by Cnut and subsequent kings, and also as personal bequests and grants from those who curried his favour. The literature slyly suggests than even more were obtained by more suspicious means.

Harold Godwinson was born sometime about 1022, the second son of Godwin Wulfnothson and Gytha Thorkelsdóttir, so he was half Danish and a cousin of the man who would become King of Denmark in 1047.[14] It has been suggested that Harold may have also been the great x 5 grandson of King Æthelred I who had reigned 866 –871, but this is totally unproven and probably unprovable.

He had an older brother Sweyn and younger brothers Tostig, Gyrth, Leofwine, Wulfnoth and possibly Alfgar. The shadowy Alfgar may have become a monk at Reims and died young. His sisters were Ealdgyth/Edith, Ælfgifu/Eadgifu and Gunnhilda. Note the mixture of Scandinavian and English names.

It may be that Godwin had an earlier marriage, as William of Malmesbury wrote that he had been married twice, but he was very vague if not downright wrong about the details and the information is suspect. No children are known of this alleged marriage, which if it occurred would probably have been 'in the Danish style' and repudiable. There were also associated rumours of former slave trading between Denmark, England and Ireland, run by either this wife or Gytha. Certainly, Godwin had contacts in Ireland.[15]

King Cnut's death in 1035 was somewhat unexpected. His own oldest son Sweyn had been with his mother Ælfgifu[16] in Norway acting as regent,[17] but being deposed had fled to Denmark where he had died in 1034. So, he was out of the English succession issue. He had been displaced from Norway by Magnus the Good, son of Ólaf Haraldson.[18] Magnus would later also become King of Denmark (*see below*).

Cnut's son by Emma, Harthacnut, was by now acting as regent in Denmark. Emma promptly manoeuvred for the throne of England on behalf of Harthacnut, but her stepson Harold Harefoot, a son of Cnut by his first wife, Ælfgifu of Northampton (although some have claimed that Cnut was not his father, or that he was a changeling) was physically in England and also laid a claim. The Witan prevaricated and split over the succession, but Harefoot gradually gained ascendancy in England, except in Wessex where Harthacnut, through Emma as his regent and supported by Earl Godwin of Wessex, was holding on. But Earl Godwin then swung behind Harefoot, and the Witan eventually consented that Harefoot became 'protector' of all England in 1037. This made things very difficult for Emma and she fled to Flanders and Harthacnut rather than Normandy, as the latter was going through a somewhat anarchic phase. If Harthacnut had promptly returned from Denmark he might have gained all England for himself, but he was pinned down defending Denmark from Magnus, the new King of Norway.

In the period of instability in 1036, before Emma fled, and possibly encouraged by letters purporting to be from Emma, but also suggested to have been a ruse by Harefoot – the content of which may have implied that they had a chance of restoration to the royal family in England – both Edward and his brother Alfred made almost simultaneous forays to England. These have been interpreted as attempts by them to regain the throne for the House of Wessex.

Edward's attempt had considerable support from Normandy, but the expected English support was not forthcoming on his landing near Southampton, and he retreated. Alfred's foray from Flanders, supported by the Flemish Count Baldwin V, aiming to meet his mother at Winchester, was intercepted in Surrey near Guildford, by Godwin's men. The *ASC(C)* says:

> But then Godwine stopped him, and set him in captivity,
> And drove off his companions, and some variously killed;[19] some of them were sold for money, some cruelly destroyed, some were fettered, some of them were blinded, some maimed, some scalped.
>
> No more horrible deed was done in this country since the Danes came and made peace here. Now we must trust to the dear God that they who, without blame, were so wretchedly destroyed rejoice happily with Christ.
>
> The ætheling still lived; he was threatened with every evil; until it was decided that he be led to Ely town, fettered thus.
>
> As soon as he came on ship he was blinded, and blind thus brought to the monks. And there he dwelt as long as he lived.
>
> And afterwards he was buried, as well befitted him, full honourably, as he was entitled, at the west end, very near at hand to the steeple, in the south side chapel. His soul is with Christ.

This act would in the future come to haunt Godwin, as Alfred's brother, Edward would never forgive Godwin's role in Alfred's death. Godwin benefitted further from supporting Harefoot in 1038 as Kent was added to Godwin's Earldom of Wessex when the sitting Archbishop of Canterbury died. From this point onwards Godwin controlled all of the south coast.

Harold Harefoot died suddenly at the age of 23 on 17 March 1040. The cause of death was possibly suspicious, but the *ASC(C)* pithily just says:

> Here King Harold died.

Negotiations between the English magnates and Harthacnut concerning the throne, undoubtedly involving Godwin, then dragged on a while, but eventually Harthacnut and Emma sailed from Flanders, just before mid-summer, with a moderately large escort of 60 or so ships to Sandwich where they received a good welcome. Harthacnut is then said to have had Harefoot's body exhumed and thrown into a fen. He had thoroughly disliked his presumed half-brother.

Harthacnut himself did not reign for long, he died on 8 June 1042. He just dropped down dead with a convulsion. He had been drinking heavily at the time. He was only 24. His short reign was not popular, even something of a failure.

There must have been some sort of premonition of disaster for during 1041 negotiations had been held for Edward 'brother of the king' to finally return from Normandy to join Emma and Harthacnut in government as co-ruler and heir presumptive. It also indicated a clear wish that Edward should be Harthacnut's successor. The *ASC(C,D)* records loyalty oaths sworn by magnates to Edward in 1041. Godwin was involved as ever in this move, but the rôle of Emma is more enigmatic. Godwin had been promoted by Cnut, had survived him and had survived his sons. Now this ambitious true survivor and master of the realm would serve Edward. Godwin, although implicated in the murder of Edward's younger brother Alfred, now supported Edward against his mother, the Queen Dowager Emma, who for her own unknown reasons had flirted with the idea of supporting Magnus. It seems her relationship with Edward was cool, if not icy. During late 1042 Godwin was instrumental in getting the pro-Norman Edward (the Confessor, son of Ælthelred II and the same Emma) supported by the Witan as King of England, instead of Magnus of Norway. The delay of his coronation until Easter 1043 has been explained as wishing to associate the crowning of Edward with this great Christian event. This might have been a 'flexible with the truth' reason. It is notable that almost immediately Edward after the coronation deprived his mother of her lands and wealth, sending a posse of three earls, Leofwine, Godwin and Siward by surprise to seize the goods:

> Because she had kept it from him too firmly

At least one source suggests that she had promised the crown and treasure of England to Magnus if he were to invade. During the reign of Harthacnut (1040

–1042) Emma instigated the writing of the three-part *Encomium of Queen Emma*, which would be later revised to record later other life events, the final entries may have been as late as 1050. Its short *Book III*, records Emma's troubles as perceived by herself during the reign of Harold Harefoot and the accession of her sons, Harthacnut and Edward the Confessor to the throne. She died in 1052 and was buried at the old minster in Winchester. The story of all Emma's 'actions' after the death of Cnut is well covered by both Stafford and O'Brien, the latter describing Emma as a Machiavellian mother. Emma's wishes would have little standing. Harthacnut had indicated his wish that his half-brother succeed him, he had obtained the support of the magnates and he was of the house of Cerdic (Wessex) the ace card in the inheritance game. The *ASC(C)* states that Edward was chosen king 'as was his natural right'.

As pointed out by Howard,[20] if Swein Estridssen had been easily available he might have been another candidate of the Anglo-Danish establishment in England for the English throne. He was also a potential heir of the throne of Denmark on Harthacnut's death, but Magnus had got into Denmark first. Swein was 'not available' because as will be explained in the next chapter, Cnut had had Swein's father, Ulf Thorkelsson[21] executed in 1026x1027 and Swein was still in exile in Sweden in 1042. Also, as we shall see Björn Estridssen, Swein's brother, had been murdered by Sweyn Godwinson years before, or he too would have been another contender.

The whole matter of the successions to the English throne between 860 and 1066 get very complex. Even after the Danish conquest some attention needed to be paid to the process of succession, which was not totally by might. There is a very well-considered paper from Ann Williams on this tricky subject which includes the role of the Cerdic (Wessex) dynasties, the differing dynamics and the roles of the witan, the support of thegns and other magnates and regnal families which examines the transitions from Edmund Ironside to Cnut, Harold Harefoot to Harthacnut, Harthacnut to Edward the Confessor and finally the competing claims of Harold Godwinson, Edgar Atheling and William of Normandy. These were all surprisingly balanced in terms of the power of a king's family, his predecessors wishes and his most powerful subjects support, all of which were required to support a king's legitimacy.[22]

Fig. 3. Arms of the Kingdom of Wessex. First seen in a 13th century manuscript. Formal heraldry did not fully evolve until the twelfth century.
CC BY SA-3.0 ex Wikipedia

Notes

1   A brother of Sigvaldi Struthharaldsen, commander of the Jömvikings based at their legendary stronghold, Jömsborg, on the Island of Wollin, an island off the coast of present-day Poland, near the German border, then under Danish control.

2   Daughter of Ealdorman Ælfhelm (possibly *PASE*'s 'Ælfhelm 15') and his wife Wulfrun.

3   This led to a family feud with Thurbrand killed by Uhtred's son, Ealdred, who in turn was killed by Thurbrand's son, Carl. This blood feud went on for decades. Finally in 1073x4 Waltheof (Eadred's grandson) cornered all Carl's sons and grandsons and killed virtually all of them.

4   Sometimes quoted as at Gillingham in Kent, but this is confused with Gillingham in North Dorset, a previous Royal manor and forest very near Penselwood.

5   The 1st Battle of Otford was in 776, between the Mercians and Men of Kent.

6   At Ashingdon, north of Southend in Essex.

7   Probably not today's Alney Island as is often thought, but a former small island in the River Severn near Deerhurst, Gloucestershire. Ola's Island is no longer to be seen, but the area where it existed is located by the river and is now called locally 'The Naight'. It is near a surviving rare Saxon chapel called Odda's Chapel dated 1056. (This was built by Earl Odda, who had replaced Earl Godwin in western Wessex when Godwin revolted). *The Survey of English Place-Names* says: 'Naight Brook, runs into the Severn at Deerhurst at a point where old flood banks seem to show the river formerly had a second channel creating an island and the name confirms that; ēgeð 'small island, ait', with initial *n* – in the modern form from an older wrong analysis of ME *atten eit* as *atte neit*... The place is called *æt Olanige* in *ASC(E,F)*, and *ASC(D)* describes '*set Olan íge wið Deorhyrste*' (Olan against or near Deerhurst). It is unlikely to be Alney Island some 7 miles further south. *Olanige* means 'Ola's island'. See http://epns.nottingham.ac.uk/browse/id/53285a8fb47fc40ab3000630 .

8   This was not suggested until after 1070.

9   There are many theories about Agatha's ancestry. She was probably related to Emperor Henry II and was possibly a daughter of King Stephen of Hungary or of Yaroslav I of Kiev (married to Ingrid Olafsdóttir of Sweden). If the latter, her sisters can be identified as married to western European kings – Ellisif to Harold III Hardrada of Norway, and Anna of Kiev was the second wife of King Henri I of France. This made her son Edgar a nephew of both Hardrada and Henri I! Agatha was an unusual name at the time and may have been after St Agatha of Sicily, whose name was derived via a SE European Orthodox root from the Ancient Greek ἀγαθή (agáthē) = good. There are also some name theories that Agatha, who went to Scotland with her children after the Conquest, introduced the names David and Alexander into the Scots' royal lines.

10   Also known as Erik of Hlàthir.

11   OE 'Cild' meant a significant young English noble.

12   He collected his pallium in 1022. The pallium is the symbol of a special relationship with the Pope and expresses the power, that, in communion with the Church of Rome, the metropolitan archbishop or bishop acquires by right in his own jurisdiction. See https://www.vatican.va/news_services/liturgy/details/ns_lit_doc_20091117_pallio_en.html

13   This is a matronymic, and it is also known as the patronymic Ulfinger dynasty.

14   Swein II Estridssen.

15   Slave trading in England, Denmark and Ireland was not uncommon at that time. Not

practised by the Normans, slavery was slowly abolished in England after the Conquest.

16   Cnut's first wife, whom he repudiated and replaced by Emma of Normandy.

17   Cnut became King of Norway in 1028x89. His first regent Håkon Erikssen was drowned at sea soon after his appointment and that is when Cnut placed his oldest son Sweyn, assisted by his first wife.

18   Who had been King of Norway 1015–1026.

19   A cemetery site was discovered at Guildown Avenue, Guildford in 1929. 220 skeletons were found, the majority (190) dating from the late Saxon/Saxo-Norman period. Many displayed evidence of violent deaths and it has been conjectured that the site it is related to this event. (*Surrey Historic Record Ref. SHHER_1629*).

20   Howard, I. 'Harold II: A Throne-worthy King' in Owen-Crocker, GR. (Ed.) *King Harold II and the Bayeux Tapestry* (2005).

21   Cnut's brother-in-law, married to his sister Estrid. Sometime after this Cnut tried to marry the widowed Estrith off to Robert I of Normandy, with the results noted in the text above.

22   Williams, A. 'Some notes and considerations on problems connected with the English royal succession, 860–1066' in *Anglo-Norman Studies 1978*, Ed. R Allen Brown (1979).

The Godwins were known for their political acumen and talent, but they were also ruthless, headstrong and troublesome.

2

Harold Godwinson becomes Earl of East Anglia and Earl Godwin quarrels with Edward the Confessor

At Edward's accession Godwin gave him a gift of a great warship, twice the size of one he had given to Harthacnut, we are told. A poem about it reads in part:

> A golden lion crowns the stern.
> A winged and golden dragon at the prow affrights
> The sea, and belches fire with triple tongue
> Patrician purple pranks[1] the hanging sail
> On which are shown the instructive lineage
> And the sea-battles of our noble kings
> The yard-arm strong and heavy holds the sails
> When wings incarnadine[2] with gold are spread...

One of Godwin's rewards for his services and his present was that his son, Harold, was made Earl of East Anglia in 1044 when he was about twenty-four. There had been no Earl of East Anglia since 1021, as Cnut was also King of Denmark and Norway, and Harthacnut had also been King of Denmark, so the area had been well protected during these times. Many Danes had settled in England during their reigns and were peaceably assimilating. They would not readily welcome new aggressive Danish invaders, but unfortunately some might now be expected, and they needed protection.

Harold was now the East Anglian representative of Edward with powers to act on his behalf in matters of law, and to raise a fyrd (army) from the earldom in war or emergency. There were extensive estates, the income from which was designed to cover the expenses of administrating the earldom, and to support Harold and his entourage in an appropriate manner for an earl.

Edward now certainly needed a strong earl in East Anglia, and a year after his appointment Earl Harold proved his strength as he led the English fleet out of

Sandwich in successful manoeuvres to discourage Magnus I of Norway (and by now Denmark), who had raised a raiding fleet.

Why Magnus? The reasons for this were twofold. Cnut had deposed Olaf II as King of Norway in 1028, but Olaf's son Magnus I, just before Cnut's death in 1035, had gained this throne from Cnut's son, yet another Sweyn, who had been placed as co-regent of Norway. Also, Magnus I and Harthacnut, who had become King of Denmark on Cnut's death, had made a tontine treaty[3] in 1038–39 which stipulated that, if either died childless, the other was to inherit the other's throne. Magnus had promptly taken Denmark on Harthacnut's death in 1042, and clearly reckoned that the deal had included England, thus posing a significant threat from across the North Sea.

Sometime after becoming Earl of East Anglia, Harold joined with Edith Swanneshals[4] as his partner 'in the Danish fashion'. She was the daughter of a significant landholder within East Anglia and the heiress to extensive lands in Essex, Suffolk and Cambridgeshire. If she was *PASE Domesday's* 'Eadgifu 24 the fair' in 1066 she held lands worth £351.26 and was lord of lands worth £176.41, the 25th largest holding in England[5]. They were together for the next 20 years and had at least seven children. One of their daughters, Gytha, married the Grand Prince of Kiev and this – if the genealogies are correct – makes both herself and her father ancestors of the present British royal family. This is discussed later.

Soon after Gruffydd ap Llewelyn became King of Gwynedd and Powys in 1039 he started to make trouble on the Welsh border and attacked Mercia at a battle at Rhyd-y-groes on the Severn near Welshpool. This was a foretaste of the trouble he would cause in the Welsh Marches over the next 24 years, although he did call on Sweyn Godwinson for some help to defend against a Welsh rival in 1045, but that did not stop another incursion near Leominster in 1052.

The earls of England needed to work together, and by 1045 no fewer than four were Godwins: Harold himself; Harold's father Godwin of Wessex; Harold's brother Sweyn of South Mercia; and Danish cousin Björn Estridssen[6] of Northampton. The other earls were Leofric of Mercia, Ralf of Hereford[7] and Siward of Northumbria. On top of this, Edward made Godwin's daughter Edith his queen in 1045.

The Godwins were known for their political acumen and talent, but they were also ruthless, headstrong and troublesome, some more than others. In 1046 Earl Sweyn Godwinson abducted the Abbess of Leominster – and it took almost a year to make him release her. We do not know if she was a willing abductee or not, but Sweyn was exiled for this offence against the church, and his earldom was split between Björn and Harold. Hákon Sweynson, of whom we shall hear later, may have been the offspring of this rather odd relationship between the abbess and the earl.

Earl Godwin's support for Sweyn during this incident strained the relationship between Godwin and King Edward. This was already difficult at times as Godwin disliked the large number of Normans that Edward had introduced into the court, and Edward had never forgotten Godwin's role in the death of his brother Alfred. The influence of Normans on Edward cannot be understated. He had lived in Normandy in exile for 25 years since boyhood and had only come back to England at about the age of 38 once Harthacnut was on the throne. He had surely acquired something of the tastes and outlook of a Norman, spoke Norman-French and must have known his Norman relations well, including his younger relative via his mother Emma, William.

He remained unmarried, but then married Edith, daughter of Godwin and sister of Harold in 1045 when he was about 43. There were no children, which may have disappointed Godwin, who may have wished to be grandfather to a dynasty.

1048 saw Harold once more in charge of the English navy, this time dealing with raiders who managed to get through and raid Essex, part of his own earldom. Meanwhile, the German Emperor Henry III was defending his own border from Magnus of Norway. Then Magnus's death saw his half-uncle, Harald Hardrada, claim Norway and fight Swein Estridssen, a cousin of the Godwin offspring through his wife Gytha, for control of Denmark. Swein won. In these confused and turbulent years, Emperor Henry had, by 1049, formed an alliance with Edward whereby the English fleet, part led by Harold Godwinson, was to contain the Danish 'pirates' by sea whilst the emperor dealt with them by land.

During all this, Sweyn Godwinson returned to England from Flanders where he had been in exile. He tried to reconcile formally with Edward, but the Witan, whose members included Harold and Björn, refused consent to this, and Sweyn was given four days' safe conduct to leave England. Before he left there was news of 'pirates' in the English Channel and the king ordered Earl Godwin to take a fleet of 42 ships, some commanded by Harold, others by Björn, to intercept them. This fleet became weather-bound at Pevensey, and Sweyn turned up and somehow persuaded Björn to accompany him, the result of which was Björn's murder. In terms of Anglo-Danish king-worthiness in England Björn was the most eligible man in England at that time as he was a nephew to Cnut and to Godwin's wife[8]. After this Sweyn was named 'nithing', that is a person of no value, and he went back to Flanders. Some of his ships deserted him, but things had gone too far and two of them were nevertheless intercepted by ships from Hastings, their crews slain, and the ships given back to the king.

Over the winter of 1049x50 Godwin tried to persuade Edward to allow his oldest son back, and this was eventually allowed, under the condition that Sweyn would undertake a pilgrimage to Jerusalem. He eventually did this after the next events of 1051 but died in 1052 at Constantinople during his return. In 1051 Edward blocked the appointment of a nominee of Godwin as Archbishop of Canterbury, and instead appointed his own favourite Norman advisor, Robert Champart, a former Abbot of Jumièges, Bishop of London since 1044. This may have been the start of new tensions with Godwin, whom Edward still held responsible in part for his brother Alfred's murder.

In the summer of 1051, Edward was visited by his former brother-in-law, Count

Eustace II of Boulogne. Afterwards, travelling back to Flanders, Eustace demanded free lodgings for himself and his men at Dover. The people of Dover refused, and there was a fight with several deaths on both sides. Eustace returned to the king to complain, following which Edward angrily summoned Godwin, and ordered him to ravage Dover to punish the people. Godwin refused to ravage in his own earldom, Edward called the Witan to judge this refusal, and added in the issue of Godwin being involved in the murder of his younger brother Atheling Alfred by Harefoot's men in 1036.

Godwin knew a trap when he saw one and gathered the Wessex fyrd, plus Sweyn and Harold with their troops. Edward in turn alerted his army plus Eustace, Archbishop Robert, his nephew Ralf of Mantes, and Earls Leofric of Mercia and Siward of Northumbria. On 1 September, whilst Edward was at Gloucester news was brought that Godwin, his sons and their army were nearby.

Godwin demanded an opportunity to refute the charges made against him concerning Alfred's murder. He also wanted Eustace to stand trial for his actions in Dover. Edward stalled, summoned the northern earls again and cried treason. Godwin's bluff was called when the Midland and Northern earls with their fyrds arrived. Civil war loomed, neither side wished to have Englishmen killed by Englishmen in battle, negotiations took place, and Godwin's army dispersed. Following this, Edward once more commanded Godwin and Harold to appear before him. They asked for guarantees of safe conduct, but Edward refused. Godwin was again in an impossible position: if he went to Edward, his safety was at risk, but if he stood his ground it could come to conflict. In the end, Godwin, Harold, and the rest of his sons were declared outlaws and given five days to leave the country.

Whilst Wulfnoth, Godwin's youngest son and Hákon, Sweyn's son[9], remained behind as hostages with Edward, Godwin, his wife Gytha, and his sons Sweyn, Tostig and Gyrth boarded ship at Bosham and went to Flanders. They remained all the winter, but whilst there they negotiated the marriage of Tostig with Count Baldwin IV of Flanders's daughter, Judith. Judith was a daughter of Baldwin and his second wife (also called Judith), who herself was a daughter of Duke Richard II of Normandy. This created an alliance and a safe haven for the Godwins.

Harold and Leofwine Godwinson had sailed from Bristol for the Norse stronghold of Dublin. Once there, Murchad, the new King of Dublin, allowed the Godwinsons to recruit mercenaries for what seemed an inevitable struggle with King Edward.

To add to the build up towards future events, the *ASC (D version only)* briefly reports a visit by the 23-year-old Duke William of Normandy and his entourage to Edward in 1051x1052 during the exile of the Godwins. This may have been a follow up to the story about the appointment of Robert Champart as Archbishop of Canterbury. Robert was a confidant of Edward and, en route to Rome to collect his pallium, he is said to have conveyed an offer from Edward of the succession of England to Duke William. He may have conveyed a promise to William of the succession during this visit, but historians disagree about whether the event even occurred and, if so, how seriously Edward meant the promise, and whether he later changed his mind[10]. It was possible that Edward could have had children. Even although it appeared that his marriage to Edith of Wessex was probably blighted by infertility or possibly a chaste political one, he could have divorced her and married again, although that would have caused difficulties with the papacy as she was an anointed Queen. Whilst the Godwins were in exile Edith was sent to the convent at Wilton and Edward must have certainly toyed with the idea of divorcing her.

In early 1051 Edward might have been drawn to the idea a Norman successor. No precedent existed for English kings to nominate heirs except of the bloodline, who were supported by consensus and acceptance of lordship by the magnates[11], but this was not the case in Normandy. In Normandy, from the time of its foundation by Rollo, it was usual for the incumbent to name his successor before his death[12]. Usually, it would have been the eldest son, but not always. The logic was that the nobles would swear an oath of allegiance to the heir before the present incumbent died. This practice of grooming the next ruler was less developed in England; although in England blood line was important there might be more than one atheling (throne worthy) candidate available . But this was how it was done in Normandy, so William would probably have seen nothing wrong with the process. Possibly, neither would Edward who had spent those long 25 years in Normandy[13].

At that time Edward also had other living male relatives – his nephews Earl Ralf of Hereford (the Timid) and his brother Walter Count of Mantes – and there was also an exiled son of his half-brother, Edmund Ironside living in Hungary, Edward Atheling – who would have had little knowledge of England.

No one wanted another Scandinavian king[14], and a return of a Viking dynasty; in any case the power struggles between the English earls would have made it difficult for any to be successful. A Norman succession would ensure that the Channel was kept closed to Vikings although things would still have been tricky with the earls.

Notes

1   Ostentatiously decorated.

2   Flesh coloured or stained with blood.

3   Tontine: By which the last survivor takes all.

4   OE. Ealdgȳð Swann hnesce = Edith Gentle Swan, although more commonly known as Edith Swan-neck.

5   From http://domesday.pase.ac.uk/. This presumes that Edith Swan-neck was 'Edith the Fair' – *PASE Domesday's* 'Eadgifu 24' as opposed to Queen Edith, who is 'Ealdgyth 3'. Significant spelling variations of English names and places are common in *Domesday*, and Edith Gentle Swan is recorded by *PASE* with 217 entries, with names varying from Eddeda to Ædgeua, with the most common variants being Eddeua (111), Eddeuae (25) and Edeua (20).

6   Nephew of Godwin's wife Gytha.

7   Edwards's nephew, son of his sister Godgifu and Count Drogo of Mantes.

8   Later his brother Swein Estridssen was similarly possibly king-worthy but twice missed his chance of the English crown, although he did become King of Denmark in 1047. For details see Howard ,I. 'Harold II: A Throne-worthy King' in Owen-Crocker, GR. (Ed.) *King Harold II and the Bayeux Tapestry* (2005).

9   Weir, A. *Britain's Royal Families – The Complete Genealogy* (2008). She quotes Hákon to be Sweyn's son via his liaison with the Abbess of Leominster.

10   There is significant historical disagreement about these events and it is noted that Normandy was not on the normal route from England to Rome, although Robert would surely have been tempted to deviate to visit Jumièges. Bates' *William the Conqueror* covers the arguments in detail.

11   Although the Danish, Anglo-Danish and Norman-Danish kings of England probably took the opposite view, although it is noted that Harold I and Harthacnut both had to coerce the magnates into consensus. Anglo-Norman Edward the Confessor's accession whilst obvious took a while to fully achieve. Before Sweyn/Cnut who ruled by conquest, succession had been by male primogeniture or fraternal and from within the bloodline of the House of Wessex / Cerdic.

12   Rollo himself passed his lordship to William Longsword a few years before 923.

13   The supporting and acceptance of lordship role of the Witan in appointing kings appears overlooked.

14   Neither Magnus nor Harald Hardrada, uncle and heir of Magnus, who both based their claim to England on the basis that Harthacnut and Magnus had agreed that if either died childless the other would have his throne, and also that he was a successor of Cnut.

15   This is the Vegetian strategy, described in the 4th century by the Roman, Flavius Vegetius Renatus, which is discussed in more detail in '*1066 and the Battle of Hastings: Preludes, Events and Postscripts*' and expounded in Gillingham, J. ''Up with Orthodoxy' – In Defence of Vegetian Warfare' *Journal of Medieval Military History* (2) (2004).

16   Shortbow and crossbow archers. It is believed that the longbow was not developed as a serious tactical anti-cavalry weapon in England until sometime around the reign of Edward I, and later in France, although it had been used by the Welsh and Scandinavians before that. The history of the longbow is, like most medieval developments, indefinite.

17   Possibly deployed by Conan II of Rennes against William in Brittany, whilst Harold was on campaign with William in 1064.

The Witan, in a political fudge, had held that the crisis of 1051 had been caused by 'bad counsellors'.

3

Return of the Godwins, the death of Earl Godwin and Harold becomes Earl of Wessex

This was all before the return of the Godwins and their gradual re-establishment of a powerbase. On 24 June 1052, Earl Godwin made a sortie from his exile in Flanders across the Channel possibly to see what support he could count on from Wessex.

After recruiting (no doubt vigorously) at Winchelsea, Rye and Hastings he retreated to Pevensey, as King Edward's fleet sallied forth from Sandwich to find him. A storm covered Godwin's further retreat to Bruges, after 'acquiring' additional ships from Pevensey, but soon after that he returned to England, landing on the Isle of Wight.

At the same time, Harold and Leofwine left Dublin with nine ships full of mercenaries. They ravaged Porlock in north Somerset and sailed up the River Severn which provoked Earl Odda, whom Edward had made responsible for the western part of Wessex. The local fyrd was called to try to remove them but failed. This was Harold's first aggressive as opposed to defensive military action, and it was a small-scale success. The Godwin brothers then sailed round Land's End and joined their father off the Isle of Wight, after which they went to Portland, Dorset where Godwin re-declared his authority as Earl of Wessex. From there the combined fleet sailed up the Channel to London, gathering men and ships (again, no doubt, from Seaford, Pevensey, Hastings etc.) as they went.

Once more Edward summoned the earls. Ralf and Odda responded, but Leofric and Siward were this time noticeable by their absence, and Edward found himself outnumbered. Arriving in London, Earl Godwin talked directly to the citizens and persuaded them to support him. As in 1051, two English armies faced each other, but Bishop Stigand of Winchester acted as an intermediary, a truce was made and a meeting of the Witan called. The missing party was Sweyn Godwinson who had died in 1052 during his return from pilgrimage.

The Witan when it met included Leofric and Siward. Godwin cleared himself, on oath, of involvement in the Atheling Alfred's death and of treasonable intent by himself and family. The Witan and the reluctant king accepted the oath.

Following this Godwin and his family were restored to their lands, although Godwin did not retrieve western Wessex from Earl Odda[1], and Edith was released from Wilton Abbey and 'restored to the king's chamber'. The Witan, in a political fudge, had held that the crisis of 1051 had been caused by 'bad counsellors' – that is Edward's Norman advisors. *Ordericus Vitalis* reports that, following the temporary eclipse of his family, Earl Godwin when restored in 1052 was somehow able to promptly dismiss Robert Champart, the controversial Archbishop of Canterbury (or at least caused him to flee). Champart may have somehow, with Edward's assistance, taken Edward's hostages, Wulfnoth Godwinson and Hákon Sweynson, with him and handed them over to the care of William of Normandy.

Stigand of Winchester was appointed as archbishop, but Robert Champart appealed to the Pope, who reinstated him. Then Champart died at Jumièges on his way back from Rome. This incident does show just how confident Godwin felt. He was clearly prepared to manoeuvre around Edward, although never to overthrow him. But a new pope still refused to recognise Stigand and removed his pallium so that he was no longer able to perform archiepiscopal functions such as the consecration of bishops. Stigand also held on to the see of Winchester and some abbeys. This pluralism had also been forbidden by a series of popes. Edward could have dismissed Stigand, but he did not.

Earl Godwin did not enjoy his return to favour for very long, for on 15 April 1053 he collapsed during a royal banquet at Winchester. He suffered a stroke and died three days later. This was with the knowledge that he would never be grandfather to a dynasty via Edward and Edith's marriage.

King Edward then made a substantial political move and appointed Harold as the new Earl of Wessex, although this did not include western Wessex until after Earl Odda's death in 1056. He also created him Dux Anglorum. This was a new title, indicating not that he had been designated heir, but the military deputy of the king.

At this point Northumbria started to cause trouble. It had always been semi-detached from the rest of England and had a residual Danish-Saxon law structure, so King Edward appointed another of Harold's brothers, Tostig, to the earldom. Undoubtedly this was with the instruction to convert the earldom to Anglo-Saxon law and align it as fully as possible with the rest of England. Earl Ælfgar of East Anglia thought that the earldom of Northumbria should have been his and his complaints riled King Edward, who promptly outlawed him some time in 1055.

Following the familiar former example of the Godwins, the discarded Ælfgar fled to Ireland where he raised a force of mercenaries which sailed to Chester. He then allied with the King of Gwynedd and Powys, Gruffydd Ap Llewellyn, to join him to attack England.

The North Welsh king, however, had another issue he wished to deal with first: Gruffydd Ap Rhydderch of South Wales. With the help of 18 shiploads of mercenaries supplied by Ælfgar, Gruffydd Ap Llewellyn raided South Wales, which resulted in the killing of his rival. They now turned on the southern Welsh Marches, the area previously known as Hwicce, but avoided conflict with Ælfgar's father, Leofric of Mercia, who incidentally was married to Lady Godiva. Ralf the Timid, Earl of Hereford,[2] was sent against them. He decided to use cavalry and suffered a monumental defeat, following which Hereford was ravaged and burnt, including its cathedral. Earl Harold was sent to sort things out but only organised the repair of Hereford and came to terms with Ælfgar.

A year later Bishop Leofgar of Hereford led an army against Gruffydd but lost a battle and his life on 16 June 1056 against the Welsh in the Machawy valley, near Painscastle, north-west of Hay on Wye. So, King Edward had to look elsewhere for a force to defend England. He called on Harold again. Earls Harold Godwinson and Leofric and Bishop Ealdred of Worcester gathered a large army, and with this at their back sat down with Gruffydd to talk. Ælfgar was reinstated as Earl of East Anglia, Gruffydd gained some borderlands, and Ælfgar accepted Tostig as Earl of Northumbria. Although it was not an ideal solution, it broke the alliance of Ælfgar and Gruffydd. This ended up with Gruffydd Ap Llewellyn recognised as King of Wales in exchange for him recognising Edward as his overlord.

Edward had started to think about his successor again, and tried to find Edward Atheling, the son of Edmund Ironside, who was by now with his family to Hungary. Bishop Ealdred of Worcester set out in 1054 to track him down but was unsuccessful. In 1056 Harold, in diplomat mode, may have travelled to visit Baldwin of Flanders and on to Cologne then to Regensberg, met the Hungarian king there, found Edward Atheling and negotiated his return to England as a possible heir for King Edward. Walker proposes a scenario for this,[3] but it is not directly recorded.

Whatever happened, Edward Atheling arrived in England with his family in 1057, coinciding with the death of Earl Leofric. Edward Atheling unfortunately died soon after arriving, before he could even meet King Edward, but he had a young son, Edgar Atheling, and other children, whom King Edward took into the royal household, under the care of Queen Edith. Earl Leofric's son, Ælfgar, succeeded him in Mercia and a new Earl of East Anglia was appointed – yet another Godwinson: Gyrth.

On 21 December 1057, Ralf the Timid, Earl of Hereford, and another potential heir died. His son Harold Ralfson was also taken into the royal household. His earldom, which covered much of south-west Mercia, was divided into three parts: Harold gained the Welsh border counties, and Ælfgar and Leofwine Godwinson split the more eastern counties.

Of all the earls of England, now only the unsettled Ælfgar was not a Godwinson.

In 1057 Ælfgar made yet another alliance with Gruffydd Ap Llewellyn of Wales, which Edward saw as a threat and banished Ælfgar. Part of the deal this time was that Gruffydd would marry Ælfgar's daughter Ealdgyth of Mercia, said to be a great beauty. Once more, Harold in diplomatic mode arranged for Ælfgar to be given back his earldom and Gruffydd some English borderlands. The alliance ended when Ælfgar died sometime after August in 1062. He was replaced by his son Edwin.

 As soon as Christmas was over, Harold, as military commander, struck at Gruffydd, not this time in response to a specific Welsh incursion, but to deal with him once and for all because of his frequent and destructive raids into England He determined to destroy him and regain the lands the English had had to concede to him over the years, and to leave the Welsh disunited once more, plus gained some of the lowlands of Gwent. Harold and his brother Tostig undertook a joint land/sea operation, which involved the fleets from East Sussex. This was a severe retribution for the trouble that Gruffydd had caused over more than 20 years. It created a terror that would be remembered for a very long time, so much so, said Gerald Cambrensis in his *Chronicles*,

> that none of the three Norman kings who followed Harold had much trouble from the Welsh.

By the spring of 1063 Gruffydd and his shrinking forces had fled inland to the fastness of Snowdonia, where he continued to harass the English, but eventually fled to Ireland. *The Ulster Chronicle or Annals of Ulster/Annála Uladh* records that in 1064 Cynan Ap Iago,[4,5] brought Gruffydd's head to Harold, who took it and laid it at the feet of King Edward. Edward's response is not recorded. An English 'mopping up' operation probably continued in Wales well into 1065.

There are yet more stories, preceding 1064, concerning the manoeuvres to secure a clear royal Wessex blood-line successor to Edward the Confessor, in the person of Edgar Atheling, grandson of Edmund Ironside (Edward the Confessor's half-brother). Hariulf of the Abbey of Saint-Riquier[6] in the *Chronicle of St. Riquier* wrote that Edward obtained an oath (perhaps by 1062x63) from his English magnates to recognise Edgar's right to succeed. This is rarely mentioned, but both Licence and Bates have recently highlighted this.

William had an undisputed but indirect female bloodline claim to the throne of England via his great-aunt, Queen Emma, who was also the mother of Edward the Confessor from her marriage to King Æthelred II. But William had not a drop of royal Wessex blood. And in the shadowy wings waited some potential Scandinavian claimants, distantly related to King Cnut, wishing to reclaim the lost Anglo-Danish kingdom. Harold Godwinson was not of English royal blood, although descended from the Danish royal family via his mother, but his sister Edith was married to Edward.

Notes

1   Earl Odda had been given western Wessex to look after following the Godwin banishment in 1051.

2   King Edward's nephew from his sister Godgifu's marriage to Drogo of Mantes.

3   In: Walker, I. Harold the Last Anglo-Saxon King, (2000).

4   Cynan ap Iago (d. about 1060), was the son of Iago ab Idwal, King of Gwynedd from 1033 to 1039. Iago was murdered by his own men, after which Gruffydd ap Llewellyn, of a different house, usurped the throne. Cynan found refuge in Ireland and later encountered and killed Gruffydd ap Llewellyn there on 5 August 1064.

5   'The son of Llewellyn, king of the Britons, was killed by the son of Iago' In The Annals of Ulster U1064.8 at https://celt.ucc.ie/published/T100001A/ .

6   This abbey, founded in 625, was situated in Ponthieu, not Normandy. Its website says 'the abbey played an important part in the preservation and transmission of knowledge until the end of the 12th century.'

Harold being at his country seat at Bosham, went for recreation on board a fishing boat.

William of Malmesbury

In history there can be multiple interpretations and explanations of what actually occurred, which we can only sift for probability.

4
Harold Godwinson's 'fishing' trip to Ponthieu: An historical 'What if?'

arl Harold Godwinson took a sea trip on the English Channel in the late spring or early summer of 1064, possibly even late summer 1065. The outcome of this voyage may have led to a key point, even the deciding factor, in William the Conqueror's decision to invade England after the death of Edward the Confessor, and the crowning of Harold as King of England in early January 1066. The voyage is one of the great mysteries of the complex preludes to the Battle of Hastings on 14th October 1066.

William of Malmesbury simply thought that Harold went fishing and was blown seriously off course.

> Harold being at his country seat at Bosham, went for recreation on board a fishing boat, and, for the purpose of prolonging his sport, put out to sea; when a sudden tempest arising, he was driven with his companions onto the coast of Ponthieu.

It is difficult to believe that he was just going on a 'jolly' or leisure fishing trip and, if so, why did he take three ships full of armed men? One can be fairly sure that he normally left the business of fishing to poor fishermen.

So just why and how did Earl Harold Godwinson take three ships from Bosham in West Sussex, and end up by chance or intention in the feudal county of Ponthieu, which lay between Normandy and Flanders on the other side of the Channel, quite a way to the east? Sea voyages could be fraught with danger, and were usually not undertaken lightly, especially by kings and earls of the realm, unless there was a particularly good reason. And if a westerly gale had blown up near Bosham surely Harold's ships would have tried to run into one of the English harbours in Sussex, including Seaford, Pevensey, and Hastings, rather than allow themselves to be blown 160km (100 miles) across a wild English Channel to Ponthieu? The simple map below (figure 4) shows the differences in direction of Normandy, Ponthieu, and Flanders from Bosham.

This is the first ambiguity of the Harold/William saga. But what were the possible causes for the trip, what were Duke William's relationships with Guy of Ponthieu and his family? What reactions and events took place in Ponthieu, Normandy and maybe Flanders, up until the time that Harold was finally met near Eu on the Norman/ Ponthieu border by Duke William and escorted to Rouen?

The *Bayeux Tapestry's (BT)* first scene shows 'Harold' in audience with King Edward at the king's palace. He is accompanied by another man, who is unidentified. An alternative explanation is that the two men were messengers, bringing the news

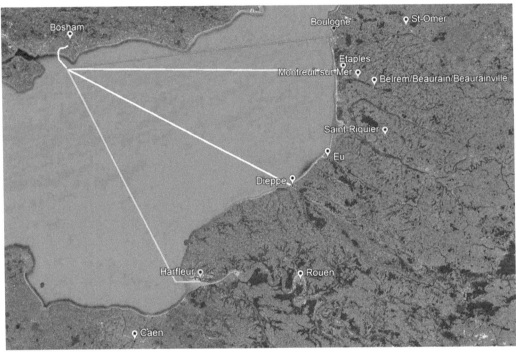

Figure 4. Straight line routes from Bosham to Normandy (white and green) and Ponthieu (pale blue) and Flanders (red), plus key places mentioned in text. Base line Google Earth Map

of Harold's impending departure to Edward, but the former must have been meant by the designer of the *BT*. After this scene Harold and his men gallop off hunting, then go to church to say some prayers, have a feast, then load up the ships and off they go. These are scenes imagined by the illustrators, we do not actually know where or if the conversation took place, nor what it was about. Clearly you would think that Harold would not have ventured out towards the opposite Channel coast without having some discussion with Edward first, or would he? And if it happened who initiated the event, Harold or Edward?

Harold might have been being sent by Edward on a diplomatic mission to either Normandy or Flanders, and if to Normandy the trip may have been related to Edward's wish that Edgar Atheling be seriously considered to be the heir apparent to England. After all, Edgar had something that was now quite rare – he was of the Cerdic/Wessex bloodline. The leading magnates of England may have been persuaded to make an oath to this effect in the previous year, as recorded in the *Chronicle of the Abbey of St Riquier* in Ponthieu. After all, Edward had taken Edgar, his sisters and a cousin, Harold Ralfson[1] into the royal household and given Edgar the title Atheling, normally reserved for the sons of kings and clearly indicating an adoption. Although Edward had had no children this would be a change of tack from what may have been a previous understanding made way back in 1051 during William's supposed visit. What is disturbing is the silence of the *ASC* for the years 1062 and 1063 about all this, has the oath to Edgar been 'disappeared'? What has not disappeared is an entry in the New Minster at Winchester's *Book of Life*[2] of the grouped names of Edward, Edith and Edgar Atheling (as Edgar clito), a fact that would have clearly marked Edgar as an adopted son and heir apparent.

In the context of Edward conferring the title Atheling on Edgar, he must have been trying to establish Edgar, who was possibly six to eight years old when he came to England in 1057, in the same way that his contemporaries did for Henry IV in the Empire and Philip I in France. In both other cases, their fathers (respectively Emperor Henry III and King Henri I of France) pre-designated them as heirs who would be supported by their mothers, Agnès of Poitou in the Empire, and Anne of Kiev in France, until they reached the age of 15. Henry IV was only five or six years old when he succeeded in 1056 and Philip I only eight in 1060. Although difficult to be precise, Edgar was perhaps seven to ten in 1062x63 at the time of an oath but certainly less than 15 years old[3] when his great uncle died.

Edgar could never have been in as strong a position as these near contemporaries, as he was a great-nephew, had partially grown up in a foreign land, may not have even spoken Old English when he arrived, and his support would have been from his almost certainly marginalised mother Agatha[4] and the perhaps not too supportive Queen Edith and her family. Edward clearly cannot have tried hard enough to develop Edgar, nor establish strong enough support for him from the time he was taken into his household – he would have needed more than the oath in 1062x3 given that the Witan was a consensual body, that needed to agree to support a candidate and accept the presumed heir's lordship, which might initially be through a regency. It may only have been a façade of consent.

Edgar would have had the support of Archbishop Ealdred of York in 1066, who was very aware of the European views on child kings and the mechanisms to strongly support them, if you had the correct people to do it. The Archbishop did in fact re-attempt to support Edgar's cause after the death of Harold, but could not rally any accord and support slipped away in the Godwinless vacuum. The Godwinsons had been too strong and their deaths and that of many English thegns and housecarls clearly left England with no leadership strength in depth after 'Hastings'. Earls Edwin and Morcar were also still young (Edwin was about 22 and Morcar 20) and relatively inexperienced. We know nothing of Atheling Edgar's character, but maybe it was not that strong and he was too easy to marginalise. Ward gives an excellent review of child kings and the wider European views on the correctness of what happened in England, including a detailed analysis of Edgar's position.[5]

The *ASC(D)* for 1066 says:

> ... Archbishop Ealdred and the garrison in London wanted to have Prince Edgar for king, just as was his natural right, and Edwin and Morcar promised him that they would fight for him, but always when it should have been furthered, so from day to day the worse it got, just as it all did in the end...

The *ASC(C)* also mentions Edgar's position as perceived by the 'people' because Abingdon Abbey had a new abbot requiring to be confirmed in post by the king:

> ...and then sent him to the Atheling Edgar because the local people thought he ought to become king,...

After William became king and heard of this he became very angry with the abbot elect and made him pay 40 marks to be reconfirmed!

But returning to further considerations of Harold's motivation for his trip, he might have wished to go to Normandy to try to get his nephew Hákon and brother Wulfnoth released. They were still there, held as hostage against the Godwin family's good behaviour by William on Edward's behalf since 1051, even though Earl Godwin had been dead for 12 years.

He might also have been going to make tentative arrangements of one sort or another to involve William as an ally in the governance of England after Edward's death. Harold was not an Atheling (a king worthy prince of royal blood), he was Edward's very able right-hand man, military leader and chief diplomat, so the discussions may have centred around a continuance of that role under or in partnership with William.

It was unlikely that he would be going deliberately to Ponthieu, which was a small buffer county between Normandy and Flanders, whose count was a vassal of William's and would have no significant influence – unless Edward was trying to build up an alliance of all the neighbouring polities around Normandy, which would have been a difficult task given all the different agendas.

About the Counts of Ponthieu

Guy of Ponthieu was a discontented vassal of William and his family was not well disposed to the Norman ruling family. There are also back and side stories to the relationship of the County of Ponthieu to the Dutchy of Normandy, and of Guy of Ponthieu with William of Normandy. Ponthieu was not a part of Normandy, but Guy had become a vassal of William's after being imprisoned subsequent to the Battle of Mortemer in 1054 (see below). There is no doubt that Guy had a family history of antagonism with William, which dated back to William's disagreements with Guy's uncle, Count William of Arques, whom the young Duke had created a count probably by 1042, definitely by 1044. William of Arques (also known as William of Talou) was the son of Duke Richard II of Normandy by Papia/Popia/Poppa, his concubine after the death of his first wife, so undoubtedly may have had his own thoughts about becoming Duke of Normandy. His older half-brothers whose mother was Judith of Rennes[6] had been dukes of Normandy: Richard III from 1026 to 1027, and Robert I from 1027 to 1035. Robert I was the father of William the Conqueror. In 1035, following the death of Duke Robert I, William of Arques had unsuccessfully challenged his young nephew William's right to succeed his father, basing his own claim on his legitimate descent from Richard II.

There was therefore more than a little tension between the two Williams. Arques/Talou had withdrawn from William's siege of Domfront in 1051–2, renounced his vassalage and went off to rebel in eastern Normandy, having already subverted the Duke's garrison at the castle of Arques.[7] William of Arques was joined in his revolt by his brother-in-law, Enguerrand II, who in 1052 had become Count of Ponthieu, which included the county of Aumale, brought into the family via an earlier marriage. To make familial matters worse, Enguerrand had once been married to Duke William's sister or half-sister[8] Adelaide, whose date of birth is very uncertain (1025x1035). This political marriage had been useful to William as Ponthieu controlled the strategically useful Abbeville on the Somme River and Montreuil-sur-Mer, then on the coast. The marriage had produced a daughter, also called Adelaide, but after the papal Council of Reims in 1049 the marriage of Enguerrand and Adelaide was annulled on the grounds of consanguinity in 1049x1050[9,10,11]

This all led to a siege of the castle of Arques by Duke William. In an attempt to relieve the siege, King Henri I of France arranged a small armed force to try to do so, but forces loyal to Duke William ambushed them at nearby Saint-Aubin-sur-Scie on 25 October 1053. In the skirmish the disgruntled Enguerrand, who was part of the raiding group, was killed.

Duke William duly recovered the castle of Arques and permanently banished William of Arques from Normandy, and Guy I (either a son or brother of Enguerrand) became Count of Ponthieu. Following this episode, Guy was then involved with King Henri of France in early 1054 in an aggressive thrust by the King into Normandy from the east, which resulted in a victory at the Battle of Mortemer for Duke William's forces. Guy was taken prisoner and held at Bayeux for two years until he swore perpetual fealty to Duke William, with the promise to supply him with the services of 100 soldiers annually, a not inconsequential financial burden. So, they became nominal allies, but begrudgingly, and it has been noted that Guy continued signing charters of the French king.

Late 1056 was a time of a flurry of diplomatic activity and jockeying for position in Europe following the death of Emperor Henry III, in October 1056. England was an interested observer of what was going on and Harold was in diplomatic mode. He visited Count Baldwin V in Flanders, perhaps whilst en route to, or returning from, a visit to Rome, which could also have involved meeting the King of Hungary and Agnès of Poitou (whilst she was acting as regent for her young son, Henry IV). This might have involved Harold in negotiations for the return of Edmund Ironsides's son, Edward, to England as a potential blood heir to Edward the Confessor, who was his half-uncle. But it also led to an interesting meeting as the recently freed Guy of Ponthieu attended a meeting in Saint-Omer arranged by Count Baldwin V of Flanders, which was also attended by Harold Godwinson and the future Bishop of Amiens, Guy, who later wrote the *Carmen de Hastingae Proelio*.

One outcome of this meeting is that on 13 November 1056, Baldwin V of Flanders approved a diploma for the Abbey of Saint Peter and Saint Paul of Ghent, and among the witnesses were both Earl Harold Godwinson and Count Guy of Ponthieu – so we know that they knew each other from well before 1064.

Another outcome was that having been found by Edward the Confessor's emissaries, Edward Atheling, sometimes known as Edward the Exile, journeyed with his family to the English royal court in 1057. This was after the due negotiations and agreement of terms, possibly involving Harold, at Regensberg in Bavaria, at Christmas, 1056, with the Hungarian King Andrew I and maybe Agnès of Poitou. Unfortunately, Edward Atheling died soon after arriving in England, before he could even meet King Edward, leaving a son Edgar Atheling and two daughters, who were to be brought up in the English court. Edward Atheling was buried with Æthelred II at old St Paul's[12] rather than at Glastonbury with his father Edmund Ironside, a symbolic means of more closely associating him, and therefore his son Edgar, with a crowned member of the Wessex royal line. The situation with respect to Edgar has already been extensively discussed above.

One daughter, Margaret, later became the second wife of King Malcolm III of Scotland, and their daughter Maud/Matilda would marry Henry I of England in 1100, bringing the blood line of Cerdic/Wessex back into the potential English succession.

We do not know how Harold's arrival in Ponthieu was 'welcomed'. Harold's three boats full of armed men are shown in the *BT* as beached on a possibly sandy shore.[13] Unless Guy was actually expecting him, it is unlikely that he would have been there to 'welcome' Harold as shown on the *BT*. But whatever happened, he was taken or made his way to the castle at Belrem,[14] now Beaurainville and formerly Beaurain-sur-Canche and, maybe, held hostage.

The end of the voyage to Ponthieu is immortalised with imagery on the *Bayeux Tapestry* (*BT*) with the associated words:

HIC: APPREHENDIT: WIDO: HAROLDVM: ET DVXIT: EVM AD BELREM: ET IBI EVM: TENVIT (L)

Here Guy (Wido) seized Harold and led him to Beaurain (Belrem) and there he held him.

Although Belrem/Beaurainville was 60km (37 miles) from the Normandy–Ponthieu border just north of Eu, it is 160km (100 miles) overall to Rouen where William is known to have been at that time. So, there would have been some delay, even with fast horses, to get the message about Harold's presence in Ponthieu to William. The messengers may have taken at least one Englishman with them as an Englishman[15] is seen pleading with William to send messengers back to negotiate and do a deal, or maybe simply to send people to collect Harold and his party and escort them to Normandy. Chronicles indicate that William eventually paid a large sum of money and gave Guy some land to hand Harold over (possibly to compensate for William having formally made his sister Adelaide Countess of Aumale, thus keeping hold of her dower land from Enguerrand). The money may not have been a ransom as has been suggested, but a reluctant gift of thanks. Harold and his companions were passed to the 'care' of William, Duke of Normandy, near Eu on the Ponthieu–Normandy border. William rode out to meet Harold in style and all (minus Guy of Ponthieu and his retinue) went on to great hospitality at William's palace at Rouen.

It is noted in the *BT* that Guy is shown riding a horse with mule's ears for this trip, maybe a mocking gesture by the designer or embroiderer to this vassal lord who dared do a deal with William. Above the exchange transaction scene there are two camels in the upper border of the *BT* (figure 5), a truly exotic animal in northern Europe at that time.

Figure 5. Camels in BT upper border (Frame 13)[16]
Bayeux Tapestry 11th Century ©Bayeux Museum.

These must have had relevant symbolism, as does much of the upper and lower borders of the *BT*, in this case probably biblical and connected to large matters of 'justice, mercy, and faithfulness'.

> Woe unto you, scribes and Pharisees, hypocrites! for ye pay tithe of mint and anise and cummin, and have omitted the weightier matters of the law, judgment, mercy, and faith: these ought ye to have done, and not to leave the other undone.
> Ye blind guides, which strain at a gnat, and swallow a camel.
> *(Matthew 23: vv 23 and 24, King James version)*

This is related to those who are scrupulous about small things but ignore higher issues. The upper and lower borders of the *BT* are filled with other classical, eastern and Christian allegories and real life scenes, with mythological figures, such as the wyverns (with their association with Harold), griffins and winged horses, as well as (amongst others) lions, camels, peacocks, bears, fish, eels, dogs, birds, plus farming and hunting scenes, pastiche illustrations of Aesop's and others' fables, as well as Halley's comet and scenes of battle and erotica, not unlike moralistic scenes carvings in early Romanesque churches. There was even 'the Hand of God'.

Amongst the identified fables are: The 'fox and the crow'; the 'wolf and the lamb'; 'the wolf and the crane'; the 'wolf and the kid'; the 'frog, the mouse and the hawk'. The first is repeated three times with the piece of cheese being dropped by the crow varying in position (it is once in mid air), the symbolism being believed to represent the tug of war between William (the crow) and Harold (the fox) with the piece of cheese they both want representing England. The last fable is a tale of false friends.

Other possibilities concerning the fishing trip

There is a remarkably interesting review of the Norwegian sources for the events of the Conquest, by Gade,[17] that confirms that, as early as 1056, Harold may have been trying to secure the early release of his brother Wulfnoth and nephew Hákon from Normandy. She also raises the 'flexibly logical' suggestion that this event might have been somehow conflated by the Norman and later scribes with the later records concerning Harold's time in Normandy in 1064 or 1065 and its objectives. The 1056 events had seen Harold in diplomatic mode, ten years before the Confessor's death, and maybe long before he might have even considered that one day he might be King of England himself.

This is just one of many attempts which have been made to understand and explain just why Harold made his fateful voyage perhaps in the late spring or early summer of 1064 (although Licence places it by dates very much later than this, after the final mopping up Welsh campaigns which stretched into 1065[18]), and the full complexities of his subsequent 'entertainment' by Duke William, and the rationale and the nature of his voyage and sojourn in Ponthieu.

The true story remains obscure, and this very obscurity gives rise to many ambiguous conspiracy theories. It was part of the Norman hagiographers' starting point to fill in the gaps favourably and construct a justification for William's claim to the throne of England.

Turning back to further explanations of the voyage, we know that both William of Jumièges and William of Poitiers claim that Harold was on a mission on behalf of King Edward the Confessor to promise the succession of the throne of England to William. The so-called briefing meeting between Edward and Harold is the first illustration of the *Bayeux Tapestry* and this ambivalent meeting fits the Norman stories, but it may not have happened quite as imagined. The context of the meeting, according to the mainly Norman sources, was associated with the dynastic succession to the English throne and was a follow up to the meeting between William and Edward way back in 1051x1052, as reported in the *ASC(D)*, when Edward may have promised his throne to William, as long as there was no more direct blood line successor (at that time it was possible that Edward might have children). Morillo[19] gives a concise selection of these sources, and he also includes a paper on naval logistics in 1066, much of which is pertinent to any voyage at that time across the Channel.

We should also make some queries about the 'rescue' of Harold from Ponthieu. Here we first assume that he was going to Normandy, not Flanders, and was certainly not on a fishing trip. Surely, if it were a planned trip to Normandy, it would have been pre-arranged between either Edward and William, or Harold and William and there would have been some sort of agenda to justify it. It would have been most strange if the second most powerful person in England suddenly arrived with three shiploads of armed men at a Norman port unexpectedly. If that had happened, the result would have been a less than friendly welcome and could well have been met with deadly force. Sea raiders were not uncommon in those day. These pirates would seize goods and/or people to sell as slaves, or would enact acts of revenge for raids in the other direction. Portsmen on both sides of the English Channel did not ask many questions; the worst was assumed about strangers. Harold may have been lucky that he was recognised and not dealt with in the same way in Ponthieu.

If William was expecting Harold, he would have been surprised that he had landed in Ponthieu and that he would have to retrieve him one way or another. After this retrieval, would Harold have been treated any differently to the way he would have been treated if he had gone directly to Normandy? If he had been expected, probably not, although it would have irritated William greatly to have to deal with Guy of Ponthieu, and Harold would have been beholden to William.

William would not have been expecting him at all if he was going to Flanders but, if that had been the case, why was Harold not escorted to Count Baldwin V of Flanders rather than to Duke William of Normandy? Was the transfer to William political and opportunistic on behalf of both Guy of Ponthieu and William, after the latter heard about matters before Baldwin? Harold's treatment in this scenario may well have been rather more underhand than if he had been expected.

The question remains: what was the mission and what was the overall objective?

If William was 'the chosen one', did Edward somehow wish to manoeuvre Harold into meeting William in person and supporting him? This fits with the conspiracy theory, suggested by Neil Clephane-Cameron,[20] which sees Harold 'set up' by Edward with an ostensibly bona fide diplomatic mission in order to place Harold in a position where William could apprehend him, and finalise their succession deal, but a Channel storm added an unanticipated twist, to which William, with his accustomed adaptability, was able to respond for his own long-term, strategic benefit.

Yet another theory exists that, for diplomatic or his personal reasons, Harold may have been seeking a new formal wife from either Flanders or Normandy to supplant Edith Swan-neck, rather than the one being proposed at that time – Ealdgyth, the reputedly beautiful young widow of the dead king of North Wales and sister of the northern earls Edwin and Morcar, and probable granddaughter of the equally beautiful Lady Godiva. This would have had English strategic benefits but may not have totally fitted Harold's plans for the future, where he might not have wanted any ties to the northern earls.

He could have been going to seek an alliance between England and Normandy, not unlike the alliance his brother Tostig had achieved with Flanders by marriage with Judith of Flanders, Count Baldwin V's sister from which Tostig gained prestige as well as an ally. This deal could also have involved a diplomatic marriage between Harold's sister, Ælfgifu and a prominent Norman magnate, perhaps even William's son, Robert Curthose, who was just old enough to marry. This may be the strange event that is referred to concerning one of the three women in the *BT*, named there as Ælfgyva, an enigmatic feature, which has never been fully explained and which will be returned to later. Eadmer says that King Edward told Harold that in going to the continent against his advice, Harold would:

> bring dishonour on the kingdom and discredit to himself.

If this were true, then the stories of Edward sending Harold on a mission to William on his own behalf must be incorrect. Edward may not have wanted Harold to parley with William to try to get his nephew and brother released, or to strengthen his hand with a prestigious marriage, and had no particular reason at this time to support a visit.

Did Edward, if he advised Harold at all, ask him to visit William on a diplomatic mission just to find out what William was thinking? And/or did he tell him not to try to secure the release of Godwin family hostages still held by William (on Edward's behalf)? Edward may have been only too happy have the hostages left in Normandy for insurance against the powerful Godwinsons.

What was he going to talk about if Edgar Atheling was the de facto heir, to whom Harold and others had sworn an oath of succession? Was Edward sending Harold to inform William of his decision to nominate Edgar as his successor? As the most powerful earl, Harold would have been ideally suited to say to William, 'Look, even

I have accepted this'. William, faced with this information, might then have decided that in this context Harold was a potential ally (both having had their ambitions displaced), and subsequently offered Harold the opportunity to retain his power if he would support William to the throne (perhaps even in a joint kingdom as per the earlier Wessex–Scandinavian examples between Cnut and Edmund Ironside and the attempted sharing between Harold Harefoot and Harthacnut, although both can be regarded as abject failures) and obtains Harold's oath to this.

On his final return to England Harold did bring back his nephew Hákon, perhaps as a sign of William's good faith, but had to leave his youngest brother Wulfnoth to remain in William's 'care'; a continuing hostage to fortune, retained as hostage for Harold's good faith. The partial exchange does indicate of some sort of deal.

Lastly, was Harold not aiming for Normandy at all and actually going on a diplomatic mission to Flanders on behalf of Edward? He had made similar trips before. Flanders was as large as Normandy at that time and its coastline extended to the Comté of Boulogne. They were reasonably good allies of the English and friendly to the Godwins, perhaps less so to Edward. If Harold was going to Flanders and had ended up there, the fateful meeting between William and Harold would not have happened and the affairs of Normandy and England would have remained separate and the alliance with Flanders may have been strengthened.

William might still have tried to invade England once he realised that he was not going to be offered the English crown, after the death of Edward the Confessor, but the motivation would have been different and not coloured by the personal animosity between Harold and William, which clearly motivated William to talk passionately to his initially quite reluctant Norman followers into supporting his ambitious and dangerous plan to invade England. His henchmen might not have cooperated.

Notes

1   Son of Ralf the Timid, Earl of Hereford.

2   British Library Stowe 944 folio 29r.

3   At that time a male reached the end of childhood (pueritia) on his 15th birthday.

4   Agatha was of central European or Byzantine origin with no grounding in the politics of England.

5   Ward, EJ. 'Child Kings and the Norman Conquest: representations of Association and Succession' in Ashe,L and Ward EJ. Conquests in Eleventh Century England: 1016, 1066 (2020).

6   Judith, daughter of Conan, Count of Rennes and first wife of Richard II of Normandy.

7   Now Arques-la-Bataille near Dieppe.

8   Adelaide's mother was likely but not definitely to have been Herlève. She is also known as Adelissa and Adelidis.

9   Additionally, at a Council of Reims called by Pope Leo IX, the marriage of Duke William to Matilda of Flanders was forbidden on the grounds of consanguinity, which seemed a bit extreme as they were third cousins once removed. They married despite this in 1050–52. In 1059 Pope Nicholas II fully legitimised the marriage in the eyes of the church. They founded the two abbeys at Caen in reparations.

10   Also, at the Council of Reims the marriage of Count Eustace II of Boulogne to Godgifu/ Goda, (sister of King Edward) was ended and Godgifu returned to England.

11   Adelaide re-married to Eustace of Boulogne's brother Lambert II, Count of Lens, who died at Lille fighting Emperor Henry III in 1054. In that year the widowed Adelaide moved to Aumale, as Countess. She received manors in East Anglia after the Conquest and later became Countess of Holderness. Her final marriage was to Odo of Champagne in 1060.

12   Largely destroyed in the Great Fire of London in 1666 and replaced.

13   Maybe near Étaples on the wide beaches at the mouth of the River Canche or a bit further up what was then a large estuary near Montreuil-sur-Mer.

14   Belrem was the old west Flemish name.

15   Englishmen are nearly always depicted with moustaches in the BT.

16   BT Frame numbers refer to the position shown in the full tapestry. As seen at https:// www.bayeuxmuseum.com/la-tapisserie-de-bayeux/decouvrir-la-tapisserie-de-bayeux/ explorer-la-tapisserie-de-bayeux-en-ligne/.

17   Gade, KE. 'Northern Light on the Battle of Hastings', Viator, Vol 28, (1997): 65.

18   These ended in August 1065, and Harold does not appear in the annals until mid to late October, just after the revolts began against Tostig. There are also some indirect dating issues concerning the Breton campaign on which William took Harold, the state of the harvest in Brittany and the subsequent ability to feed William's army and keep it in the field, which point to 1065.

19   Morillo, S. (Ed.) The Battle of Hastings, (1996).

20   Personal communication.

This Englishman (Harold) was distinguished by his great size and strength of body, his polished manners, his firmness of mind and command of words, by a ready wit and a variety of excellent qualities.
But what availed so many valuable gifts, when good faith, the foundation of all virtues, was wanting?

Ordericus Vitalis, *c.*1075–1143

5
Harold Godwinson in Normandy

There is no good English contemporary record of these events, so the following words come with a health warning: that the sources were Norman.

After taking Harold and his men to Rouen, William would have entertained Harold and his senior companions with generous hospitality, the start of a velvet-gloved 'internment'. The *BT* shows in the border above their first significant meeting two peacocks (figures 6 and 7) with the one over Harold displaying its tail feathers, impressing its rival.

Figure 6. Peacocks in *BT upper border(Frame 14)*
Bayeux Tapestry 11th Century ©Bayeux Museum.

William must have seen an unexpected opportunity to discuss his claim to the English throne, with someone who could, under the right circumstances, help make it happen.

He upped the welcome, presumably making it more than obvious that he expected Harold to stay awhile. Out of gratitude for his rescue from Ponthieu Harold was in a difficult position, and might have felt obliged to humour his host, at least for the time being, whilst realising that he would not be able to get away at a time of his own choice. He would have welcomed the chance to retrieve his relatives amicably, and this would in any case take some time to negotiate. The time that William and Harold spent together, their actions and discussions provide food for much speculation, as we have seen only too clearly in the last chapter.

William clearly showed off the Norman war machine, perhaps to induce some circumspection into Harold. Did the talks centre around discussions about some sort of alliance between England and Normandy, with and without strategic marriages, and release of hostages? Did they discuss whether or not William was still in the running for the throne of England, or if Edgar Atheling was now the heir apparent? Or possible roles for Harold if William was accepted as King of England? Or some kind of power sharing?

William of Jumièges says Harold was with William 'for some time'. They would have hunted and hawked together, and William took Harold on an expedition to Brittany which aimed to undermine the Breton Duke Conan II. This was when these two powerful men would have been able to size each other up. Harold will have seen Norman cavalry and battle tactics in action. The BT shows Harold rescuing two men from the quicksands around the River Couesnon estuary on the Normandy – Breton border, showing his personal bravery, and the Normans raising a siege of Dol castle.

Figure 7. William and Harold's first discussion *(Frame 14).*
Whose peacock was proudly displaying his fine feathers, Harold's?

The greyscale images of the *BT* here and below are extracted from Montfaucon, Abbé B. de, 'Les Monumens de la Monarchie Françoise' Vol. II (1730)
From the Collection numérisées de la bibliothèque de l'INHA, Open License

But Conan II was wily, making a strategic bare-earth retreat,[1] so eventually William could not feed his army and had to return to Normandy not having unseated Conan. If it had been used this was a tactic Harold would have not used in wars against the Welsh and perhaps he should have carefully noted its effect on the outcome in actually preventing a battle. Both Harold and William would have seen something of each other's strengths and weaknesses. Harold may have been lulled into a sense of false security, perhaps somewhat misplaced as he was seeing the Norman use of cavalry and castles in war. Something he should also have carefully noted.

Somewhere along the line William knighted Harold, which it is suspected was just seen as an honorary knighting by Harold, but was of much more significance to the Norman, and seen as an act of homage. William then turned to negotiation about the throne of England, a move that must have severely disconcerted Harold, no matter what his motives, pressing Harold to support his bid. There were undoubtedly carrots, probably with the offer of one of William's daughter's (Adeliza?) hand in formal marriage to Harold, balanced by the marriage of one of Harold's sisters (see figure 8 – possibly Ælfgifu/Ælfgyva?) to one of William's senior magnates, and the final release of both Hákon and Wulfnoth.

Figure 8. Was Adeliza/ Adela/ Ælfgifu/ Ælfgyva part of the deal? *(Frame 15)*

Note the architecture, quite different from other buildings depicted in the BT*, and the overt sexual imagery. Two wyverns** belching fire are depicted under the tower feature (only the left one is shown)
Bayeux Tapestry 11th Century ©Bayeux Museum.

*Some have suggested it could have represented Wilton Abbey
**Wyverns are usually shown in pairs on the BT. Those belching fire can be seen in the lower border just before Harold is handed over to William; just after this scene; and as horses are landed at Pevensey. Did they represent Harold's displeasure? The bestiary of the BT is complex.*

If Harold had supported William's cause the retention of Harold's lands would have been an important discussion point, possibly an extension of Harold's already vast estates in England and a continuing position as 'Dux Anglorum'? Underlying the discussion was the prospect that Harold might never be allowed to return to England without some sort of deal. This deal would need to be sealed with an oath. The question has always been is was this taken voluntarily or by stealth on hidden holy relics (figure 9)? The English and Norman stories differ.

It is impossible to know the true final words of the oath, what it encompassed and if it was taken under severe mental duress, voluntarily after a generous mutually beneficial deal, or by subterfuge. We know what would be claimed later by each side. Release of the Godwin hostages was important to Harold, less so to King Edward who perhaps had lingering doubts about the Godwinsons and their motives and was happy to leave them with William. To William they were good bargaining chips in the above scenarios.

The oath was a strong enough one for William to release Harold's nephew Hákon as a token of good faith, but Harold had to leave his brother Wulfnoth hostage in token of his own good faith, an effective enough hostage to satisfy William. The fact that William released Hákon, Harold's nephew is interesting. It could be that William was demonstrating good faith in some sort of deal. He retained Wulfnoth, Harold's youngest brother, which must have been because he did not quite trust Harold. Harold, of course, would eventually gamble with Wulfnoth's life.

Was it a good enough deal for Harold seriously to consider keeping? Harold now fully knew of William's arrogant and audacious ambition. The question is, was Harold now an enemy or an accomplice of William? What if William had proposed that Harold support him as King of England, with a guarantee that he would hold on to his position, or alternatively share power with William, pushing Edgar to one side? *Ordericus Vitalis* even writes that William offered half of England and the hand of his daughter Adeliza/Adela if Harold helped William become king. This would have led to a completely different situation in England. The structure of English governance would almost certainly have been maintained and not been wiped out by large numbers of Normans and others, usurping vast quantities of lands as rewards as they did after the Conquest. Norman influence would of course have been much increased, but not been overwhelming, and the two or more centuries of Anglo-Norman imperial elitism,[2] and terrible rapines in England might have been avoided. England would have been unrecognisably different.

What if Edgar Atheling was going to be proposed to the Witan and elected king? He would have been underage and would have required a regent or regency council, this would certainly have involved Harold and probably Queen Edith plus or minus their brother Tostig and maybe others. William would not be involved in the governance of England, but it would be important that he was a friendly, or at least neutral, ally, preferably the former. But he would have had to discard the old idea from 1051 that Edward had picked him as heir reinforcing it in a message via Robert of Jumièges. This scenario might have been helped by a strategic marriage perhaps between one of Harold's daughters or Atheling Edgar's sister, Margaret, to William's son Robert (although they were all young, that did not seem to matter in those

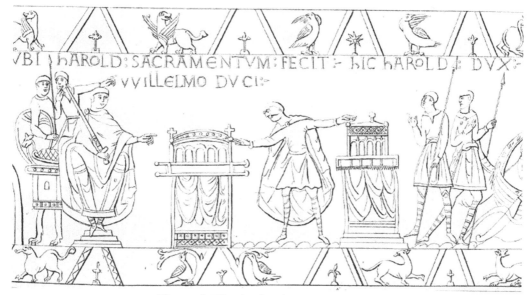

Figure 9. The Oath taking *(Frame 23)*

days). William himself was happily (we are told) married to Mathilda of Flanders and would not even consider divorcing her and making a new marriage, as (amongst many other matters) it would have mightily upset her father and his neighbour Count Baldwin V of Flanders and attracted aggressive attention from Flanders as well as the King of France. It would also have very much disturbed the papacy who, after some negotiation, had legitimised William and Mathilda's consanguineous marriage in the first place.

Even with Edgar on the throne, Harold might have been formally offered marriage to William's daughter Adeliza/Adela to tie him more closely to William and elevate his prestige in an Anglo-Norman alliance, but conversely this might have weakened his overall position of power in England as Dux Anglorum in an English regency agreement. Once Edgar came of age he would have his own ideas and may have favoured Tostig. What would England have been like then? Maybe the continuation of Wessex kingship, with strong Danish connections of its leading earls would have aligned England back within the Scandinavian sphere as Norman influence waned.

Notes

1   This might not have been the full truth. It is possible (from Poitiers reporting) that the harvest was late and local crops were not yet ready for consumption.

2   The situation was of course more thought-provoking than this simile implies. The intermingling of peoples, cultures and self-perceptions that resulted from the Conquest of 1066 is very well analysed in Thomas, HM. The English and The Normans: Ethnic Hostility, Assimilation, and Identity 1066–c. 1220 (2002).

These two great brothers of a cloud born land, the kingdom's sacred oaks, two Hercules, excel all Englishmen when joined in peace.

Vita Edwardi Regis, about 1068

6

Return to England: Until the death of Edward the Confessor

O n his return to England,[1] Harold seems to have picked up where he left off, being the right-hand man of Edward. He must have reported back to Edward, but there is no contemporary English record about this. Harold looks rather contrite on the *BT* in this scene. A few sources hint at Edward's concerns, and Harold himself must have been greatly conflicted in his thoughts and maybe very angry.

What if Edward died whilst Edgar Atheling was still quite young, but accepted as king? Clearly Harold or the Queen, his sister Edith, could have been regent during Edgar's minority, Harold would still be Dux Anglorum, or there could have been a regency council including a reconciled Tostig, who was apparently somewhat favoured by both Edward and Edith.

The *Vita Edwardi Regis,* by an anonymous author, completed in about 1067x1068 and probably commissioned by Queen Edith can give some unverifiable clues concerning Harold and Tostig. The *Vita* describes both as 'brave, handsome and strong', but Harold was the taller, with great stamina, calmer and perhaps more intelligent. Tostig may have been somewhat more inflexible and sterner. Both tended to keep their plans to themselves and could disguise their intentions. There is an intimation that Edith had hoped that Harold and Tostig would work together well. For much of the time they had done so, such as when dealing with Welsh matters and campaigns. The *Vita Edwardi Regis* says about Tostig.

> Earl Tostig himself was endowed with very great and prudent restraint although occasionally he was a little over-zealous in attacking evil – and with bold and inflexible constancy of mind. He would first ponder much and by himself the plans in his mind, and when he had ascertained by an appreciation of the matter the final issue, he would set them in order; and these [plans] he would not readily share with anyone. Also, sometimes he was so cautiously active that his action seemed to come before his planning; and this often enough was advantageous to him in the theatre of the world. When he gave, he was lavish with liberal bounty and, urged by his religious wife, it was done more frequently in honour

of Christ than for any fickle favour of men. In his word, deed, or promise he was distinguished by adamantine steadfastness. He renounced desire for all women except his wife of royal stock, and chastely, with restraint, and wisely he governed the use of his body and tongue. Both [brothers] persevered with what they had begun: but Tostig vigorously, Harold prudently; the one in action aimed at success, the other also at happiness. Both at times so cleverly disguised their intentions that one who did not know them was in doubt what to think. And to sum up their character for our readers, no age and province has reared two mortals of such worth at the same time.

Tostig had been appointed Earl of Northumbria in 1055 to succeed Earl Siward, even though he had no local connections. There was some controversy about the appointment, and it created a long-standing rivalry with Aelfgar, at that time Earl of East Anglia and his sons, as they believed they had seniority, and that too many Godwinsons were in earldoms. Aelfgar should probably have been appointed to this larger and more important earldom, which would have stopped Aelfgar's festering resentment and kept the previously discussed events on the Welsh border between 1055 and 1064 calmer.

Tostig strongly and generously supported the church in Durham and managed to sternly balance Northumbrian local rivalries and blood feuds, helped by 200 housecarls, until about 1063, after the earlier Welsh campaigns, when he may have wished to replenish his coffers. Northumbria was a difficult earldom to manage. Also relationships with the Scots had become more difficult from about 1058 with increasing numbers of raids from the north, which Tostig tried to deal with diplomatically with King Malcolm III, going as far as creating a 'brotherhood'. None the less, when Tostig and Judith went off on a long trip to Rome in 1061, Malcolm swept into Cumbria and subjugated it.[2] The Scots also harried Lindisfarne. The increased Scots proximity would not have been well received by the thanes of Northumbria as the earldom became even more vulnerable to raids, now not just from the north, but also from the west with Northumbria becoming exposed in its south-west i.e., Yorkshire.

Concerning the Northumbrian thanes' family feuds and rivalries it seems that having somehow kept some distance from these until 1063, Tostig was drawn into them, curbing the power of some local landholders through intrigue and murder, and his men are described as having used rough arbitrary justice to enforce tax collections. He then introduced a big tax increase in 1065 – a major error of judgement. This, along with the actions involving deaths of rival descendants of senior kinfolk and inappropriate promotions of others, not to mention the Scots dimension, kicked off a widespread revolt, involving nearly all the thanes of Northumberland and Yorkshire [ASC(D)].

In October, the angry thegns seized and occupied York. At Tostig's hall they seized weapons and raided the treasury and killed Tostig's retainers, chasing some as far as Lincoln. They took back what they deemed theirs by right, then declared Tostig an outlaw and sent for Morcar, the younger brother of Earl Edwin of Mercia, to be the new earl. Led by 'earl' Morcar they were joined at Northampton by Earl Edwin. The choice of Morcar was clever as Edwin, who already held Mercia, and Morcar were both sons of Ælfgar, and not big fans of the Godwinsons. They had no strong roots in Northumbria, but the stakes and potential rewards were high. The insurgents moved south looking for recompense from Tostig's holdings outside Northumbria.

Tostig was with King Edward in Wiltshire. Harold was sent to meet the rebels at Northampton and later at Oxford. After he had discussed the issues with the rebels, he concluded that it was impossible for Tostig to remain Earl of Northumbria as he had completely lost all local support. Harold returned to the king, counselled in the Oxford Council of 28 October against military action against Morcar and his thegns and acceptance of the rebels' demands. Edward was very angry, as Tostig was a favourite, but was finally swayed by his counsellors as the situation could only have been resolved by significant military force, which would have seen a civil war between north and south. As we have seen before, Englishmen did not like fighting wars with other Englishmen and weakening the nation.

Tostig continued to argue with King Edward and would never forgive his brother, whom he believed had betrayed him and he made all sorts of accusations against him, including that Harold had fomented the northern rebellion that had led to his dismissal – one so serious that Harold had to clear himself by oath. Tostig left with his family for Flanders with his family a few days later, he went to Bruges to join his brother-in-law, Count Baldwin V. The author of the *Vita Edwardi Regis* just did not know what to write.

For the first time since Sweyn Godwinsons' death, the Godwin family was divided. Harold went to Northampton and told Morcar he was now officially Earl of Northumbria, and that the rebels were pardoned. Morcar then appointed Oswulf/ Osulf II as deputy north of the Tyne, whose grandfather Uhtred had been the Earl of Northumbria murdered by Cnut. This strengthened Morcar's position.

Harold also probably finalised an arrangement to marry Morcar and Edwin's sister Ealdgyth to strengthen his English alliances, and particularly to embrace the north. This removed the possibility of a marriage to a Norman or Flemish princess, which also would limit his future options. Harold, Edwin and Morcar divided up Tostig's Northumbrian estates between themselves in late 1065. Any possibility of reconciliation with Tostig had gone, replaced by implacable hostility.

New kings of England (if not intrusive Danes) were traditionally drawn from the royal Wessex[3] family but not necessarily by primogeniture. The probable blood heir was Edgar Atheling and, normally, with the support and acceptance of his lordship by the Witan, he might have succeeded with Queen Edith as regent during his minority and with Harold 'Dux Anglorum' continuing as his military aide and advisor, running the country for a few years until the youth was old enough to rule on his own. Edith may have wished under those circumstances to restore Tostig at this stage to help run the country. But he could become a potential ally of Edgar, who might have been easily manipulated to Harold's disadvantage and even led to Harold's downfall. Would this have even been possible given the breakdown between Harold and Tostig?

There were aggressive claims from Harald Hardrada of Norway as well as William of Normandy, the latter having a family claim through his great-aunt, Emma of Normandy, and a consecrated Queen of England, and believing he had been promised the throne of England, although he had no Cerdic/Wessex blood.

The meeting of the Witan and celebrations of Christmas saw all five earls, the Archbishops of York and Canterbury, eight bishops and many leading thegns gathered in London. After Christmas many would have left to return to their homes. On 5 January 1066 Edward, on his deathbed, summoned the Witan which may have been somewhat depleted and not very representative of the provinces. He had been semiconscious for several days but had roused. He is said to have commended his kingdom and the protection of his queen to Harold and bound his Norman servants to take oaths of loyalty to Harold.

Whatever was said, the Witan, still somewhat depleted, met almost immediately afterwards and clearly had a majority to support Harold as King of England. He was crowned in much haste before anyone could change their minds (figure 10). We do not know what was said.

What has never been clearly ascertained, and probably never will be, is whether

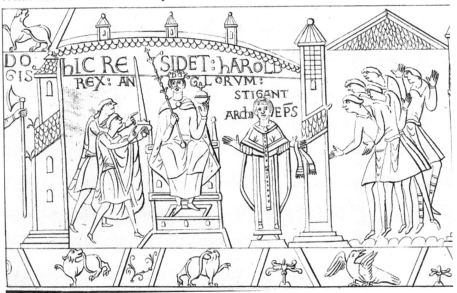

Figure 10. The crowning of Harold. Archbishop Stigand of Canterbury is shown, but the anointing was performed by Archbishop Ealdred of York *(Frame 30)*

Harold had manoeuvred long term for this, in one or other of the possible scenarios described above, or any other way. The events of the last few months, including the loss of Tostig, may have been the decider for him and the plans he might have for England. He had been Edward's right-hand man, protector, advisor, diplomat and fixer for over ten years: he clearly had great ability, but was he 'throne worthy'? Did Edward really mean to hand over to him as a caretaker, not as king? Would Harold have been just as content serving Edgar Atheling?

He had broken the apparent oath to support Edgar and would not have wished to serve William, nor co-rule with William if he had made such a deal in 1064x5. Licence says,

> By taking the throne from Edgar Atheling, Harold changed the rules. William decided that he had as much right as Harold. As an opportunist he did what he could get away with and made up his excuses later.

It could be argued that William had more right than Harold, as he was at least within Edward's extended family via Emma, and also son of Edward's blood-brother, Robert of Normandy. His deficit was neither a Cerdic/Wessex nor Anglo-Danish royal blood line. On the other hand, Harold could claim a relationship via his mother to be a cousin of the Danish king, but he too was not of Cerdic/Wessex royal blood, in fact his English heritage was from the third rank of English nobility.

Neither line was strong. What then came into play in January 1066 was the wish of the dying king (which is not absolutely clear to us from this distance in time) and the support of the available magnates. Ann Williams at the end of her paper on the English royal succession comments:

> ...the possession of a valid title was useless without the ability to acquire – or compel – allegiance... Both Harold's and William's conflicting claims in 1066 is not that one or the other (or both) were true or false. Both were accepted as valid at that time. Harold's on 6th January when he was 'chosen' and consecrated and William's at Berkhamsted in November, when he in turn was chosen by the English magnates (what was left of them) as their king and lord... It was a pragmatic acceptance of the realities of power that made William 'full king over England'.

Notes

1   This is impossible to date accurately, Heimskringla says it was Spring 1065, but this is not reliable. Towards the end of his Welsh campaign, at the end of July 1065, Harold organised construction of a hunting lodge at Portskewet, Monmouthshire. He must have considered that this area was subdued. Caradog Ap Gruffydd Ap Rhydderch had other ideas and destroyed it and ravaged the neighbourhood in late August 1065, without suffering any recorded major reprisals. [ASC (C,D)]. As noted by Licence, Harold is not recorded in the annals between August and mid-October, just after the Tostig affair started. Accordingly, the August – October 1065 gap might have been the period that Harold was in Ponthieu and then Normandy.

2   Cumbria had been brought under English control by the previous Ealdormen of Northumbria; Uhtred, Eric of Hlàthir and Siward.

3   Also called the House of Cerdic, named after the founder, and first Saxon King of Wessex

By taking the throne from Edgar Atheling, Harold changed the rules. William decided that he had as much right as Harold.

Tom Licence, 2020

In 1066 with the weakening of the old Wessex line of kings, the grandson of a Sussex thane, with a Danish mother, became King of England. Then, from across the seas, he was defeated on the field of Battle by the great-great-great-grandson of an outlawed son of a Norwegian jarl.

7
King for 40 weeks and one day: The Battles of Fulford Gate, Stamford Bridge and Hastings

arold Godwinson was crowned King of England on 6th January 1066. He died in battle on 14th October 1066, 40 weeks and one day later.[1] Ealdred, Archbishop of York, crowned Harold. (Stigand of Canterbury was still under interdict: so it may not have been a mistake but Norman propaganda that the *BT* depicts the devious Stigand performing the coronation rites, thereby raising the question of its validity).

A little later Harold formally arranged to marry Ealdgyth, described by William of Jumièges as a considerable beauty, and daughter of Earl Ælfgar, sister of Earls Edwin of Mercia and Morcar of Northumbria, granddaughter of Lady Godiva (Godgifu) and Earl Leofric, and widow of the Welsh King Gruffydd ap Llewellyn. This considerably strengthened Harold's political ties with middle and northern England. His wife of many years 'in the Danish fashion' Edith Swan neck was 'set aside'.

The main contemporary English source – the *Anglo-Saxon Chronicle* – observes a prudent silence about Harold's elevation, but later English writers such as *John of Worcester* and Roger of Howden (the latter drawing on the much earlier work *Historia Saxonum sive Anglorum post obitum Bedae* (a Latin account of the years 734–1148 compiled from the *Historia regum* attributed to Symeon of Durham and from Henry of Huntingdon's *Historia*) say that Edward before his death chose Harold for his successor. William of Malmesbury says,

> He [Harold] said, that he was absolved from his oath, because his [William's] daughter, to whom he had been betrothed, had died before she was marriageable.

The half-English Ordericus Vitalis has a lot to say:

> There is no doubt that Edward had bequeathed the realm of England to

his kinsman William, Duke of Normandy, announcing it, first by Robert [Champart], Archbishop of Canterbury, and afterwards by Harold himself, and, with the consent of the English, making the duke heir to all his rights. Moreover, Harold had taken the oath of allegiance to duke William at Rouen, in the presence of the nobles of Normandy, and doing him homage had sworn on the holy relics to all that was required of him....

This Englishman was distinguished by his great size and strength of body, his polished manners, his firmness of mind and command of words, by a ready wit and a variety of excellent qualities. But what availed so many valuable gifts, when good faith, the foundation of all virtues, was wanting?

Returning to his country, his ambition tempted him to aspire to the crown, and to forfeit the fealty he had sworn to his lord. He imposed upon King Edward, who was in the last stage of decay, approaching his end, by the account he gave of his crossing the sea, his journey to Normandy, and the result of his mission, falsely adding that Duke William would give him his daughter in marriage, and concede to him, as his son-in-law, all his right to the throne of England. The feeble prince was much surprised at this statement; however, he believed it, and granted all the crafty tyrant asked.'

After this Malmesbury records:

William, in the meantime, began mildly to address him by messengers, to expostulate on the broken covenant; to mingle threats with entreaties; and to warn him, that ere a year expired, he would claim his due by the sword, and that he would come to that place, where Harold supposed he had firmer footing than himself.

Harold again rejoined, concerning the nuptials of his daughter, and added, that he had been precipitate on the subject of the kingdom, in having confirmed to him by oath another's right, without the universal consent and edict of the general meeting, and of the people: again, that a rash oath ought to be broken; for if the oath, or vow, which a maiden, under her father's roof, made concerning her person, without the knowledge of her parents, was adjudged invalid; how much more invalid must that oath be, which he had made concerning the whole kingdom, when under the king's authority, compelled by the necessity of the time, and without the knowledge of the nation.

Besides, it was an unjust request, to ask him to resign a government which he had assumed by the universal kindness of his fellow subjects, and which would neither be agreeable to the people, nor safe for the military.

William of Poitiers says that shortly before the Battle of Hastings, Harold sent William an envoy with a message admitting that Edward had promised the throne to William but argued that this was over-ridden by Edward's deathbed promise to Harold. In reply, William did not dispute the deathbed promise, but argued that Edward's prior promise to him took precedence. It seems that in Normandy he might have been correct, but this was England.

Harold needed to be sure of the support of the leaders of Northumbria, including that of Oswulf II of Bernicia who was subordinate to Morcar, so by marrying the sister of Earls Morcar and Edwin he had also reassured northern England that Tostig would not be welcomed back. He also created Waltheof Siwardson Earl of Northampton – an area somewhat larger than Northamptonshire is today, in the south-east midlands – and reconfirmed the positions of Edward's Norman civil servants.

The story from after early January 1066 is that of the preparations on both sides of the English Channel, and of other related events on the North Sea, leading up to the three sequential battles in England of Fulford Gate, Stamford Bridge and, finally, Hastings. Conspiracy theorists may like to ponder the dating of these near simultaneous attacks. Was it pure chance or was there was any coordination between William and Harald Hardrada and if coordinated how was it planned at a time when communications were so difficult over a distance of about 1750 km (1100 miles), although it has been argued that communications, presumably by sea, between Rouen and Oslo, were better than we imagine. It does seem very unlikely and there is no record to support such an hypothesis. The Channel clock had been set ticking by William's anger in January 1066 and the North Sea clock by Tostig's incitement of Harald Hardrada maybe a few months later. The end date for both would have been set to avoid dangerous storms at sea in late autumn and winter.

In May Tostig returned to England. After landing on the Isle of Wight he raided eastwards along the south coast to Sandwich, 'recruiting' sailors from the Channel ports as he went. Harold called out the English fleet plus the Wessex fyrd and Tostig moved on. He turned northwards and continued raiding along the coast of East Anglia and Lindsay attacking a place called 'Brunemue' (in Gaimar, *Estorie des Engles*[2]), possibly Burnham, and named 'Brune' in *Domesday* – then via the Humber, into an area under the control of Earl Edwin. Together Morcar, the new Earl of Northumbria, and his brother Edwin of Mercia expelled the weakened Tostig. Much of his army was lost after this, and the pressed boatmen from the south coast whom he had forced into service during his south coast raids, deserted after Morcar prevented Tostig landing on the north coast of the Humber. He retreated to Scotland with only 12 ships remaining. He was allowed to stay there all summer and was assisted and re-supplied by King Malcolm III.

Harold remained well informed about William's actions across the Channel, and all summer of 1066 and held ready the fyrd and navy around Hampshire and the Solent, the area in his opinion where a landing was most likely, but Harold had to stand down his army and navy on or about 8 September 1066. The men were at the end of their period of service and harvests had to be gathered in. It was also getting late in the year, with increasing storms in the English Channel which would have made a crossing inherently more of a gamble.

Meanwhile Tostig plotted with Harald Hardrada, who had his own ideas about becoming King of England, the outcome being an invasion of Northumbria and the battles of Fulford Gate and Stamford Bridge. We have the *Heimskringla (The Chronicle of the Kings of Norway)* by Snorri Sturlason (*c.* 1179–1241) to give us the Norwegian version of the events. Snorri's tale was written down more than 150 years after the event and is based on oral histories; therefore, it is entertaining but regarded as an unreliable source (except where it agrees with the *ASC*). Interpretations of the events it describes enter and confuse later stories, but there is so little mention of the events in the north of England in the post-Conquest Norman chronicles – after all the Normans had no wish to praise Harold, or by allusion diminish their triumph, that we do need to consider the *Heimskringla*.

Below, where there are direct extracts from Snorri, they are prefixed {S} so that the reader is aware of their provenance. The *Heimskringla* tells us that Harald Hardrada had over 300 ships, the *ASC(C) version* says, 'a very great raiding ship-army', the *E version* agrees with 300, *John of Worcester* says 500.

Hardrada's force had set off from Solund on the Sognafjord in Norway, probably sometime in August, travelling via the Shetland and Orkney Islands where, we are told, he dropped off his wife and daughters on Orkney 'for a holiday', picked up reinforcements and met yet more reinforcements from Iceland before meeting Tostig, possibly in the Firth of Forth or on the River Tyne. The Norwegian army was added to by Tostig's force which with King Malcolm III's help he had managed to enhance somewhat in Scotland.

After joining forces, Hardrada's and Tostig's forces landed at the Cleveland district in the River Tees area in early September 1066.

{S} When king Harald was clear for sea, and the wind became favourable, he sailed out into the ocean; and he himself landed in Shetland, but a part of his fleet in the Orkney Islands. King Harald stopped but a short time in Shetland before sailing to Orkney, from whence he took with him a great armed force, and the Earls Paul and Erlend, the sons of Earl Thorfinn; but he left behind him here the Queen Ellisif, and her daughters Maria and Ingegerd.

Then he sailed, leaving Scotland and England westward of him, and landed at a place called (ON)Klifland [*Cleveland*]. There he went on shore and plundered and brought the country in subjection to him without opposition. Then he brought up at (ON)Skardaburg [*Scarborough*], and fought with the people of the place. He went up a hill which is there, and made a great pile upon it, which he set on fire; and when the pile was in clear flame, his men took large forks and pitched the burning wood down into the town, so that one house caught fire after the other, and the town surrendered. The Northmen killed many people there and took all the booty they could lay hold of. There was nothing left for the Englishmen now, if they would preserve their lives, but to submit to king Harald; and thus he subdued the country wherever he came. Then the king proceeded south along the land, and brought up at Hellornes [*Holderness*], where there came a force that had been assembled to oppose him, with which he had a battle, and gained the victory.

So, we are told by Snorri that Harald Hardrada and Tostig had raided down the north Yorkshire coast, with skirmishes at Scarborough, and a small battle with the local forces at Holderness, which are estimated by Laport[3] to have taken place on or about 12 – 14 September. They then sailed up the Humber estuary as far as Riccall on the River Ouse, fully invading the earldom of Northumbria on or about 16 –17 September (Laporte).

> {S} Thereafter the king sailed to the Humber, and up along the river, and then he landed. Up in Jorvik [*York*] were two earls, earl Morukare [*Morcar*], and his brother, earl Valthiof [*Waltheof*],[4] and they had an immense army. While the army of the earls was coming down from the upper part of the country, King Harald lay in the (ON)Usa [*Ouse*]. King Harald now went on the land, and drew up his men.

The northern earls, Edwin of Mercia and Morcar of Northumbria, failed at the Battle of Fulford Gate on 20 September to repel the invaders. York, which may have had some residual Danish sympathies, then surrendered rather than be ravaged, and promised to support Hardrada and Tostig against Harold Godwinson. A few days later Hardrada arranged a meeting with the citizens for the next morning for the delivery or exchange of some hostages, just in case, so to speak. Little was he to know that he would only hold York for another 24 hours (figures 11 to 15).

Fulford is sometimes thought of as a minor battle. This cannot be so, for it must have caused significant losses for the northern English army. It may be that if Edwin and Morcar had known that Harold was on the way, they might have instead retreated behind the walls of York and awaited reinforcement.

> {S} When king Harald [Hardrada] saw that the English array had come to the ditch against him, he ordered the charge to be sounded, and urged on his men. He ordered the banner which was called the 'Landravager' to be carried before him, and made so severe an assault that all had to

Figure 11. The panel from the Fulford Tapestry[5.6] showing Harald Hardrada and Tostig entering York . Image courtesy © Chas Jones

give way before it; and there was a great loss among the men of the earls, and they soon broke into flight, some running up the river, some down, and the most leaping into the ditch, which was so filled with dead that the Norsemen could go dry-foot over the fen. Then the king advanced to take the castle and laid his army at (ON)Stanfordabryggiur [*Stamford Bridge*]; and as king Harald had gained so great a victory against so great chiefs and so great an army, the people were dismayed, and doubted if they could make any opposition. The men of the castle therefore determined, in a council, to send a message to king Harald, and deliver up the castle into his power. All this was soon settled; so that on Sunday the king proceeded with the whole army to the castle, and appointed a Thing [*meeting*] of the people without the castle, at which the people of the castle were to be present. At this Thing all the people accepted the condition of submitting to Harald, and gave him, as hostages, the children of the most considerable persons.

The *ASC(C)* says,

many of the English were slain, drowned or put to flight and the Northmen had possession of the place of slaughter.

A second Thing was arranged with Hardrada early on Monday morning, where King Harald was to name officers to rule over York, to dispense laws, and bestow fiefs. We do not know the precise dates of the initial Norwegian landing, or the precise

Figure 12. The Stamford Bridge Tapestry[7.8] Panel 1:
Harald Hardrada and Tostig enter York and messengers tell Harold Godwinson the
news of the Viking invasion. Messengers gallop off to enlist the army
© Battle of Stamford Bridge Tapestry Project 2021

date on which Harold received that news. However, once he heard about the events happening near York, Harold Godwinson had to head north with an army that he hastened to gather, but with a strong core of housecarls. He would gather more support en route (figure 13).

He had a problem with the English fleet. If he had had enough ships, Harold

Figure 13. The Stamford Bridge Tapestry. Panel 2:
The English army sets off and Harold receives with dismay news of the defeat of
Earls Edwin and Morcar at Fulford Gate and the fall of York.
© Battle of Stamford Bridge Tapestry Project 2021

might have avoided much of the fatigue of his troops, as well as the logistic problems of a march to the north. The English fleet had been backing up the army, having been on watch in the Solent all summer, and had also been stood down. It had been sent to London, but unfortunately lost many vessels as it made its way around the south coast during late summer storms, the same that had prevented William of Normandy from crossing the Channel earlier. The losses from Harold's fleet may have been one reason that the king did not sail with his army en masse for the north instead of making the arduous overland journey.

It was likely that the core of Harold's throng was composed mainly of mounted warriors in view of the remarkable speed they were able to achieve in getting to Yorkshire. He managed to travel some 185 miles (300 km) in only four days, an extraordinary feat. He followed the quickest route via Ermine Street, and north of Lincoln took the alternative inland route to avoid a fording of the Humber. On the way he must have recruited from the areas he passed through, and then rallied his own and the remnants of Edwin and Morcar's army at Tadcaster on the Sunday 24 September [ASC(C)].

Although there had been losses from the fleet, some ships were available to Harold and some soldiers may have enshipped, as the ASC(C) writes (OE) 'lið fylcade' (marshalled the fleet) when talking of the mustering at Tadcaster – so a few ships may have sailed up the River Wharfe and become trapped there. Given favourable winds and tides a voyage could have taken about three days. Jones confirms this interesting interpretation:

> 'that some English ships had reached Tadcaster on the River Wharfe, which joins the River Ouse south of Riccall, before the Vikings got there.'

Presumably, some ships had been sent north from the depleted navy as a precaution once it had returned to London from the Solent, or as soon as news had reached Harold Godwinson of Hardrada's and Tostig's landings at Cleveland. If so, this might indicate that Harold may have had rather more than four days' warning of their arrival, but that he may initially have thought that it was just a Viking raid, rather than a full-scale invasion. It is also possible that the ships were based on the Humber and retreated in front of the invaders up the Wharfe, then were unable to re-enter the Ouse, as the confluence was blocked by Hardrada's ships.

Harold's arrival near York was unexpected. He could have been expecting to need to attack York, but fortunately found York undefended, thanks to the deal that had been done. No doubt he 'forgave' the citizens of York their acceptance of an offer they could not refuse from Hardrada. He was able to engage Hardrada and Tostig the next day. Hardrada was clearly caught by surprise. He had sent one third of his army back to the ships at Riccall, and many of his soldiers were unarmoured (it was reported to have been a hot day). Instead of an exchange of governance details with the cowed citizens of York he met a rather angry Harold Godwinson.

> {S} 'A Thing [*meeting*] was appointed within the castle early on Monday morning, and then king Harald was to name officers to rule over the town, to give out laws, and bestow fiefs. The same evening, after sunset, king Harald Godwinson came from the south to the castle with a numerous army, and rode into the city with the good-will and consent of the people of the castle.'

King Harold Godwinson went on to soundly defeat the Norwegians and their allies on 25 September (*John of Worcester* and *ASC(D)* say 28 September, *ASC(E)* says 29 September) at Stamford Bridge, a few miles east of York. Harold's success was helped by his use of cavalry – and as noted many of Hardrada's men were without their armour, as they had been caught by surprise. Harold Godwinson used 'hit and run' tactics throughout the battle – much as the Normans were to do three weeks later at the Battle of Hastings. Was this a lesson Harold had learnt in Normandy? If so he obviously could not use these tactics on the battlefield at Hastings, possibly because of his lack of cavalry there.

> {S} 'King Harald Godwinson had come with an immense army, both of cavalry and infantry ... Twenty horsemen rode forward from the Thing – men's troops against the Northmen's array; and all of them, and likewise their horses, were clothed in armour. One of the horsemen said, "Is earl Toste in this army?" The earl answered, "It is not to be denied that ye will find him here." The horseman says, "Thy brother, king Harold, sends thee salutation, with the message that thou shalt have the whole of Northumbria; and rather than thou shouldst not submit to him, he will give thee the third part of his kingdom to rule over along with himself." The earl replies, "This is something different from the enmity and scorn he offered last winter; and if this had been offered then it would have saved many a man's life who now is dead, and it would have been better for the kingdom of England.
> But if I accept of this offer, what will he give King Harald Sigurdssen for his trouble?" The horseman replied, "He has also spoken of this; and will give him seven feet of English ground, or as much more as he may be taller than other men."

Figure 14. The imagined meeting of Harold with Tostig his brother, and Hardrada, before the battle of Stamford Bridge, 1066
Via archive.org from: *The Story of the Norman Conquest.* Maclise, D. (1866)

Now the battle began. The Englishmen made a hot assault upon the Northmen, who opposed it bravely. It was no easy matter for the English to ride against the Northmen on account of their spears; therefore they rode in a circle around them. And the fight at first was but loose and light, as long as the Northmen kept their order of battle; for although the English rode hard against the Northmen, they gave way again immediately, as they could do nothing against them. Now when the Northmen thought they perceived that the enemy were making but weak assaults, they set after them, and would drive them into flight; but when they had broken their shield-rampart the Englishmen rode up from all sides, and threw arrows and spears on them.

Now when King Harald Sigurdssen saw this, he went into the fray where the greatest crash of weapons was, and there was a sharp conflict, in which many people fell on both sides. King Harald then was in a rage, and ran out in front of the array, and hewed down with both hands ... King Harald Sigurdssen was hit by an arrow in the windpipe, and that was his death-wound ... before the battle began again Harald Godwinson offered his brother, Earl Toste, peace, and also quarter to the Northmen who were still alive; but the Northmen called out, all of them together, that they would rather fall, one across the other, than accept quarter from the Englishmen.'

So, Harald Hardrada was already dead, and Tostig was killed in the final stand, having according to this report being twice offered terms to surrender by Harold (figure 14). Very few Vikings escaped back to Scandinavia.

The *ASC(D)* reports:

> But Harold let the king's son, Edmund, go home to Norway with all the ships. He also gave quarter to Olave [*Olaf*], the Norwegian king's son, and to their bishop, and to the Earl of the Orkneys, and to all those that were left in the ships;[9] who then went up to our king and took oaths that they would ever maintain faith and friendship unto this land. Whereupon the King let them go home with twenty-four ships.[10]
>
> As the English recovered after the Battle of Stamford Bridge, Harold's concerns about Duke William resurfaced with the news of William's landing in eastern Sussex (figure 15), and he hastened south again, leaving Morcar and Edwin to sort things out in Northumbria, and standby against any further incursion.

**Figure 15. The Stamford Bridge Tapestry. Panel 12:
Harold sends the remnants of the Vikings packing, feasts but then is informed
of the Norman Landing at Pevensey.**
© Battle of Stamford Bridge Tapestry Project 2021

It is not relevant at this point to reprise in depth William's preparations to invade England and why he ended up landing at and around Pevensey and then establishing his secure bridgehead on what was then a Hastings Peninsula. Much detail of this is covered in *1066 and the Battle of Hastings*.[11] But in summary William crossed the English Channel from St. Valéry-sur-Somme with a fleet of perhaps 700–1000 ships, an army of around 7000 men, with provisions, horses, and equipment, and even a couple of prefabricated timber castles. The fleet left Saint-Valery on the falling tide after 15.00, landing around and east of Pevensey Bay on the rising tide from about 09.00 the next morning.[12] The land and sea movements around this time are shown in Figures 16 and 17.

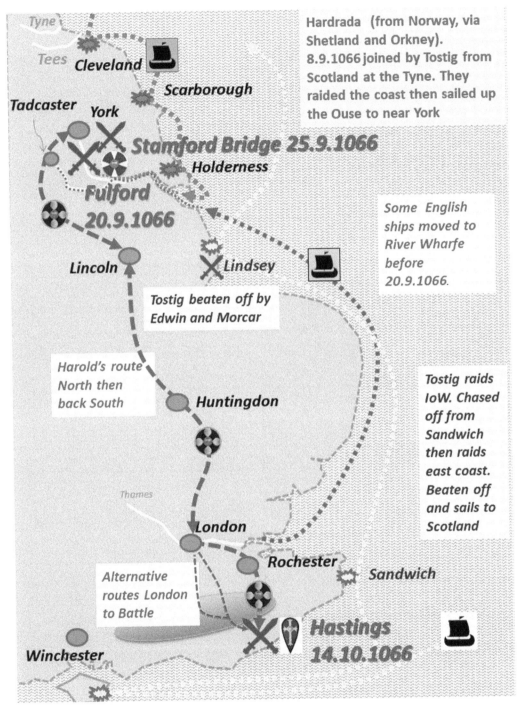

Hardrada (from Norway, via Shetland and Orkney). 8.9.1066 joined by Tostig from Scotland at the Tyne. They raided the coast then sailed up the Ouse to near York

Some English ships moved to River Wharfe before 20.9.1066.

Tostig beaten off by Edwin and Morcar

Harold's route North then back South

Tostig raids IoW. Chased off from Sandwich then raids east coast. Beaten off and sails to Scotland

Alternative routes London to Battle

Stamford Bridge 25.9.1066
Holderness
Fulford 20.9.1066
Tyne
Tees
Cleveland
Scarborough
Tadcaster
York
Lincoln
Lindsey
Huntingdon
Thames
London
Rochester
Sandwich
Hastings 14.10.1066
Winchester

Figure 16. Harold's, Tostig's and Hardrada's movements in England, the English Channel and the North Sea related to the battles of September and October in 1066
©BDHS

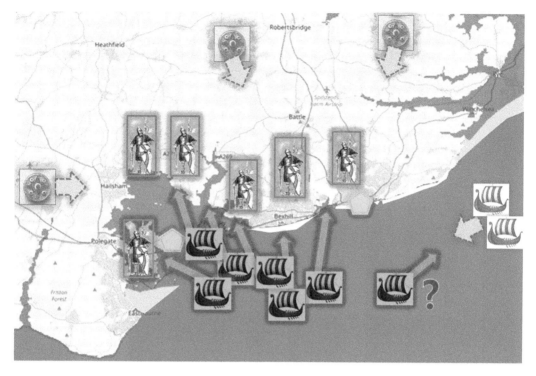

**Figure 17. The Landing zone and possible directions of English response.
Blue pentagons = temporary castles** © BDHS

My colleague, Hugh Willing, a retired senior British army officer, has spent a considerable amount of time walking around the Hastings and Battle area, considering the historic geography, and assessing the ground and has given a military explanation of the situation, as follows: Once landed without incident William proceeded to build a defensive wooden fort possibly somewhere north of present-day Pevensey, or within the old Roman fort, in order to protect his flank and his landing sites from any attack.

The army occupied the Hastings peninsula, and erected a further temporary wooden castle at Hastings, probably sited just west of the present Hastings town centre, this would also have protected the smaller havens. From the castles William would have been able to dominate the region for about 25 miles around. This area would have provided the army and its horses with food, particularly as the harvest had only just been gathered. We know from previous studies[13] (figure 18) that the most productive areas for foraging would have been from just north of Pevensey Bay to the ridge line between Fairlight and Battle.

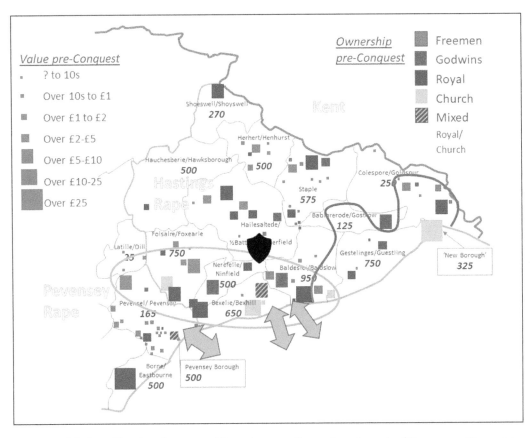

Figure 18. Supplies for the army. The zone north-east and east of Pevensey Bay was clearly the best area for foraging as it is the most productive, valuable (and populated) area, this is within the green oval. Green arrows show landing and resupply routes. The red line approximately outlines Fécamp's manor which was relatively untouched.
Modified from diagram in Foord, K. *BC to 1066* ©BDHS

The vital dominating, easily defended, ground was the ridge of land from Fairlight to Telham (near Battle) on the approach to present day Battle. This had to be held, to prevent interference with his landing and supply routes, and to buy time to consolidate against a serious attack from the English.[14] Any attempt to remove him could be observed and any ad hoc attempts to dislodge him could be fought off. He had the advantage and time to dictate where the coming fight would be held. There was an additional advantage in that much of the area was well known to the Normans as the Norman Abbey of Fécamp had owned a large manor east of Hastings since the days of Cnut, as outlined in red in figure 18.

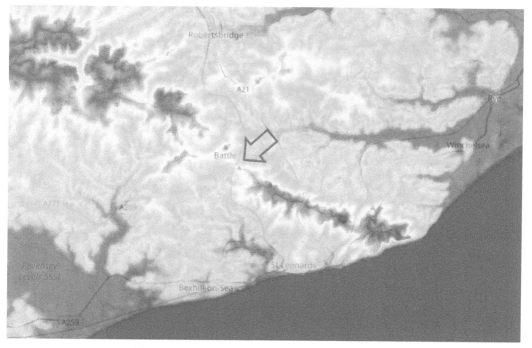

Figure 19. Topographic map of the Hastings area.
The pinch point just south of Battle is arrowed
Extracted, and modified from https://en-gb.topographic-map.com/maps/du6e/East-Sussex/

The ground off the ridge to the north extending to the higher Wealden ridge led to a natural saddle and a pinch point (figure 19) between two watersheds, with marshy ground both east and west, which he had to secure if he was to breakout from the base he had established, but this was also the place where the English had their best chance of stopping him.

Once past this pinch point William would have been able to fan out and bypass other obstacles such as Caldbec Hill. The ground therefore dictates the site of the battle and the 'vital ground' for the Normans was the approach across the saddle and the rise to what is now sometimes called Senlac[15] Hill where Battle Abbey is sited. The bridgehead was also the best place to defend after the battle against any follow up attempts to push the Normans into the sea.

We do not know exactly when Harold arrived back in the south – it is some 250 miles (400km) from Stamford Bridge to Battle, just north of Hastings – but he would have come by horse using the quickest route, and once again reinforced en route and from around London. This was another great feat, though probably not achieved at quite the speed of the journey north. He may have arrived in London on or about 5th October, where he stayed gathering what army he could for about a week. We do not know exactly how many fighting men Harold was able to bring all the way from the north, or collect on the way, or what condition they and their horses were in.

What was available of the navy was sent to the seas off Hastings to try to prevent Norman provisioning and reinforcements arriving, but the depleted English navy may not have been too much of a nuisance to the Normans.[16] Although the *Carmen (vv318–320)* notes:

> Per mare, per terram prælia magna parat.
> In mare quingentas fertur misisse carinas,
> Ut nostri reditus præpediatur iter. (L)

> *By sea and by land he is planning great battles*
> *He is said to have sent 500 ships to sea*[17]
> *To hinder our voyage back.* (Morton and Muntz)

It has been noted that the English used no cavalry and few archers at Hastings although the *Heimskringla* says that they had used horsemen with success at Stamford Bridge. Cavalry was certainly not a traditional method of fighting in England, but perhaps Harold had noted Norman prowess in this matter from his stay in Normandy and would have prepared counter measures. It is possible that they had lost many horses at Stamford Bridge and/or their horses were 'blown out' after that arduous journey to Yorkshire, followed by a pitched battle, plus the return, and were thus in no condition to be used. Neither were archers very numerous in the English army which is unexplained.

Rallying at London, Harold is believed to have marched prematurely southwards towards Hastings on 11 October without waiting to gather his full potential strength, reaching what became Battle on the evening of 13 October. His haste may have been to ensure that he caught and trapped William whilst he was within the Hastings peninsula. William had had two weeks to develop the peninsula into both a bridgehead and highly defensible position. This of course would mean that William would have to fight to get out via the pinch point at Battle.

The route of Harold from London toward Hastings has received little consideration by historians, perhaps because the sources are almost silent on the matter. Even after 600 years, the old Roman road network was still the main route and Lemmon[18] held that Harold was faced with two options: either that from London towards what is now Lewes (a section of this road can still be visited south of the A264 at Holtye, East Sussex) from which, in the vicinity of Maresfield, he would turn east on to the Uckfield–Rye ridgeway to Caldbec Hill (98km, 61 miles); or London to Rochester, then turning south via Maidstone and Bodiam to Cripps Corner where he would turn west onto the Rye–Uckfield ridgeway to Caldbec Hill (103km, 64 miles). Based to a degree on excavations conducted by BDHS at Bodiam, which showed continuous use of the Roman road into the medieval period, Lemmon favoured the eastern route. The texts which are available have nothing or do not help in this debate. The *Carmen (vv321–322)* contains an imagined generic approach of Harold and his army:

Quo graditur, silvas planis deducit adesse,
Et, per quæ transit flumina, sicca facit. (L)

Where he goes he appears to lead forests (of spears) into open country,
And he makes the rivers through which he passes run dry

(Morton and Muntz)

Neil Clephane-Cameron[19] has pointed out that these lines or something similar can be found in various classical and other texts when describing the movement of armies, to indicate their large size. Rivers running dry can be literal when thousands are foraging, gleaning water and food from any available source, especially around the Mediterranean, a natural focus of the ancient classical texts with which the Carmen's author, Guy, Bishop of Amiens, will have been very familiar. 'Forest of spears' is likewise a common classical period simile for 'a large army of men carrying spears'. Guy just reused the phrasing, which should not be overinterpreted.

There is a strategic weakness in the 'eastern' route in that, if it fitted with his strategy, it potentially left William clear to exit the Hastings peninsula and strike out west – toward the ancient capital of England, Winchester, with Harold's army then in pursuit. Pillaging as he went and supplied from the sea, it offered an escape route if needed as well as the attractive possibility of both a return to William's 'Plan A' (if his original intention had been to sail directly from Dives to the Isle of Wight, then use it as a base from which to attack Winchester), and the psychological victory which the undefended sack of the ancient capital would achieve. Earl Godwin had used the Isle of Wight in 1052 as a secure base on his return from banishment, from which to pillage far and wide, and both William and Harold will have been entirely aware of its strategic importance.

A 'western' route by Harold (London to Maresfield) would have had the effect of checking any such move and thus left William bottled up in south-east Sussex, only able to choose between A) movement by land along the narrow gap between the Andreadsweald and the Rye Camber with the English in hot pursuit until finally he ran out of land at Dover, B) re-embarkation and return to Normandy or C) stand and fight. That William was aware of this possibility was the fact that he had built a wooden fort and left a garrison at or near Pevensey, to protect this flank, and could block the narrow route north of the Pevensey embayment.

Dunlop[20] considered a third route – that of a pre-Roman track way which became the London–Rye Road (via Tonbridge) and would have been upgraded to a main route by 950. He favoured it as presenting the shortest route for Harold to take.

If Harold's instructions to the southern fyrd had been promptly followed (as it appears they were) or indeed if local commanders had already taken their own initiative, then it is possible that William was already bottled up in the Hastings peninsula with local English units established at the nodal point of Caldbec Hill. In such a case Harold could use the eastern route with confidence.

Much as we may conjecture, identification of the route that Harold took from London to Hastings is a problem to which there appears no definite answer. Harold found and bottled up William's army still encamped on a fortified Hastings peninsula, and there was no question of William's army moving out without engaging in battle, except by sea.

Harold's brother Gyrth may have offered to lead the English army at Hastings and advised less haste and different tactics. Ordericus Vitalis writes that Gyrth said,

'It is best, dearest brother and lord, that your courage should be tempered by discretion. You are worn by the conflict with the Norwegians from which you are only just come, and you are in eager haste to give battle to the Normans. Allow yourself, I pray you, some time for rest. Reflect also, in your wisdom, on the oath you have taken to the Duke of Normandy. Beware of incurring the guilt of perjury, lest by so great a crime you draw ruin on yourself and the forces of this nation, and stain for ever the honour of our own race.

For myself; I am bound by no oaths, I am under no obligations to Count William. I am therefore in a position to fight with him undauntedly in defence of our native soil. But do you, my brother, rest awhile in peace, and wait the issue of the contest, that so the liberty which is the glory of England, may not be ruined by your fall.'

Harold's rush may have been an attempt to catch William whilst still on the Hastings peninsula. In this he succeeded, whichever route he chose for the march from London. But please note the strategy described by Willing above. William may have been content to sit in his firm bridgehead and let the English come to him.

Despite all the above adventures, the English were sufficient in foot-soldier numbers to fight a long battle on 14 October, and to come close to victory, but in the bloody end they failed to keep the battle field bottleneck corked (Fig.20) and then drive the Normans into the sea. Even if they had the last task would have been far from easy given the Norman's preparation time.

The Battle of Hastings which took place on 14 October 1066 has been much written about with variable accuracy, usually presented with a rarely justified air of certainty. Judgement is required to assess the reliability of each interpretation, but the basic outline of the battle is agreed upon: Duke William of Normandy led an invading army of Normans, Bretons and French/Flemish; King Harold II led the defending English army; Duke William made numerous attacks which failed to break the static English shield wall, on at least one occasion narrowly averting disaster when the Bretons on his left flank retreated.

The battle, unusually for battles at that time, lasted all day, albeit with inevitable natural pauses not recorded in the sources e.g., to enable the Normans to replenish their supply of arrows, William and Harold to review their tactics and both armies to refresh and reform. Neil Clephane-Cameron has described the end of the battle in more detail below, and in its entirety.[21]

Gillingham[22] argues that the final breakthrough was a direct assault on the less steep Norman right flank, along the line of the ancient trackway, constrained by steep slopes to the right, which prevented an outflanking manœuvre (figure 21a).

Clephane-Cameron is more circumspect, pointing out that the ridge profile has much changed since the battle, with the building of the abbey and subsequent quarrying, cultivation and road and house building. He also considers that the English line had been shortened to the west following large English losses after chasing falsely fleeing Bretons, and that subsequently the Bretons gained a foothold there.

This opened an opportunity for a final phase of simultaneous flank and direct frontal attacks, the English left flank being stormed by Norman cavalry led by Eustace of Boulogne (figure 21b), which then led on to the Malfosse incident, when many Norman cavalrymen feel into a deep ravine when chasing the fleeing English.

Recently some notes left in the BDHS Archive by Col. Charles Lemmon have resurfaced. He had researched with the Greenwich Observatory the timing of the moon-set on the exact day of the battle and found that it was 15.55 in the late afternoon – so on that day in 1066 there was no moonlight after the sun set. In October 1952 when the moonset was at an identical time on the date he calculated to be the equivalent day in 1066 he undertook some experimental history to see how well a mounted warrior could see the terrain. He was riding his horse and he assessed how well he could see. He noted that by 17.15 light was failing, by 17.30 only large obstacles could be avoided, and half an hour later it was only safe to ride at walking pace. At 18.15 it was dark and at 18.30 intensely dark. So, pursuit of the fleeing English would have been very difficult after 17.30. No wonder so many Norman horsemen fell into the unseen Malfosse ravine.[23]

The theories about the end of the battle above are two of the better-informed analyses, but as always there are almost as many ideas about the exact placements of William's various contingents on the battlefield and the tactics of the final assault as there are books about it, but whatever actually happened, the English shield wall was finally broken.

The battle had been won by the Normans and Harold and his brothers as well as many other English thanes and lesser folk were killed. Harold was undoubtedly dead. A slab within the foundations of the former abbey church, on the site of its high altar, is said to mark the position of his death (figures 22 and 23).

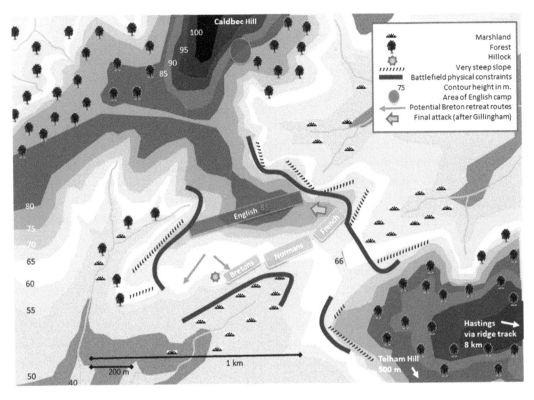

Figure 20. The final battle at the bottleneck or 'pinch point' , showing the narrow physical constraints of the accepted battlefield © *BDHS*

Figure 21a. The final assault on the English left flank as perceived by Gillingham © BDHS

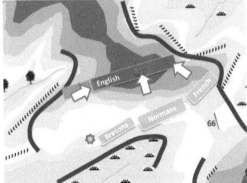

Figure 21b. The final assaults as described by Clephane-Cameron. © BDHS

The English right flank depletion allowed infiltration by Bretons combined with a Norman led cavalry assault on the English left flank, and a final frontal attack

Figure 22. A slab marks the traditional site of the high altar of Battle Abbey church, the spot where Harold fell. The abbey church site is outlined by gravel. St. Marys Parish Church in the background. Photo ©Keith Foord

Figure 23. Flowers and wreaths are very often left on the slab by visitors, particularly around 14th October and after a battle re-enactment. Here an arrangement includes a wyvern flag. Photo courtesy © Hugh Willing

The *ASC(D)'s* terse pronouncement on the subject, probably written shortly after the event, well articulates the predominant message of the *BT*, that Harold was killed and the English defeated, because of the sins that all the English had committed by allowing Harold to become king :

> 'There King Harold was killed, and Earl Leofwine his brother, and Earl Gyrth his brother, and many good men. And the French remained masters of the field even as God granted it to them because of the sins of the people.'

Some postscripts should be perhaps be considered about Harold's brothers and his own strategy:

Tostig:

Did Harold really twice offer Tostig the chance to escape with his life at Stamford Bridge as described by Snorri? Where would Tostig have fitted in if he had accepted? This might have changed English tactics leading up to 'Hastings' if Tostig had also been involved but might not have changed the final outcome.

Gyrth and strategy:

Why did Harold not take up his brother Gyrth's offer to lead the fight against the Normans at Hastings whilst he gathered reinforcements to enable a 'battle avoidance or 'Vegetian' strategy[15]' or further engagement and/or diplomacy if necessary?

One can only think that his involvement in warfare against the Welsh had not given him the full experience needed to deal with larger scale, well evolved, Norman tactics which included many archers[16] and well-rehearsed cavalry use, the latter seemingly somewhat despised in England, but which had also evolved from Vegetian strategy.

Use of scorched earth tactics, which would have been truly terrible for the people of south-east England, might have enabled Harold to deprive William's army of sustenance and later engage William in a further battle, win or buy him off. Harold may have had observed such tactics, or the contemplation of such tactics[17] in Brittany, but was he reluctant to use such devastating strategy on his home soil with the effects it would also have on his own people? As far as we are aware he had never used these tactics during his military exploits which had been mainly against the Welsh. Even his final assault with Tostig on North Wales was aimed at subjugation by terror and hostage taking rather than wanton destruction and led to a recognition by the Welsh of English overlordship.

Harold wins?:

England would have continued to develop its own identity and language…. Although another Danish invasion might have happened sometime, and/or perhaps the Scots would have subsumed Northumbria.

Animosity and humanity:

Harold's personal feelings against William, and his reluctance to inflict wholesale destruction on his own people, in order to starve the Norman army, may have been his undoing.

Notes

1   *ASC(A)* for 1066 says 'Here passed away King Edward, and Earl Harold succeeded to the kingdom and held it 40 weeks and one day, and here came William and won England, and here in this year Christ Church burned, and here a comet appeared on 18 April.' (Christ Church refers to the old Anglo-Saxon cathedral at Canterbury, the destructive fire is dated 1067 in the modern calendar).

2   British Library: Royal 13A xxi ff.40–150

3   Laporte, J. 'Les opérations navales en Manche et Mer du Nord pendant l'année 1066'. *Annales de Normandie.* 17e année No.1 (1967)

4   The *Heimskringla* is definitely erroneous on this point confusing Earls Edwin and Waltheof. However, Waltheof Siwardson might have been present.

5   The Fulford Tapestry has six panels, covering the period from the landing at Scarborough to the entry to York (http://www.fulfordtapestry.info/).

6   Stitched by a team involving Chas Jones and with the help of Jan Messent who advised on the design.

7   The Stamford Bridge Tapestry has 15 panels, 12 of which cover the period from the invader's entry to York, via the Battle of Stamford Bridge to the packing off back to Norway of the survivors of the invading army. The battle covers panels 6 to 11. (http://stamfordbridgetapestry.org.uk/gallery.php)

8   Designed in the style of the Bayeux Tapestry by Chris Rock, Chairman of the Battle of Stamford Bridge Historical Society after an idea by the late Tom Wyles and stitched by a team of volunteers under the direction of Shirley Smith. One of the stitchers has additionally produced a quilt covering the entire 1066 story.

9   Later stories say that Tostig's sons, Skuli and Ketil, were also in this group and they settled in Norway, well looked after by King Olaf III. *Heimskringla* says, 'There came also with Olaf over the West sea Skuli, a son of Earl Toste, and who since has been called the king's foster-son, and his brother Ketil Krok. Both were gallant men, of high family in England, and both were very intelligent; and the brothers were much beloved by King Olaf.' Skuli became an ancestor of later Norwegian kings.

10   Maybe 25 or 20 (*John of Worcester*). They came with about 300 ships.

11   Foord, K. and Clephane-Cameron, N. *1066 and the Battle of Hastings, Preludes, Events and Postscripts.* (2021), which covers the historic geographic aspects of William's preparations and choice of landing site.

12   The tides for any time and date can be calculated accurately, as can sunrise and sunset, moonrise and moonset, phases of the moon and eclipses in any part of the World. Some of the very few items of historical information that can be regarded as totally accurate.

13   Foord, K. *BC to 1066* (2020).

14   As Clephane-Cameron comments there was some local English activity.

15   A neologism first penned by *Ordericus Vitalis*, and popularised by Freeman. The borough created by the monks of Battle Abbey soon after 1070 and nearest the abbey was Santlache (CBA) after OE. sandlacu (a sandy brook), easily corrupted to Norman French sang lac (lake of blood).

16   *Ordericus Vitalis* says it was 70 ships, which could have been significant – the naval movements after the landings are a little considered issue in the histories. Surely William would not have burnt his boats, as some have implied, and further stores and reinforcements would have been arriving with ships going back and forwards across the Channel, when weather allowed, and standing by to resist a possible attack from an English fleet.

17   Guy of Amiens is often prone to hyperbolic exaggeration in the *Carmen*, 500 is most unlikely.

18   Lemmon, CH. *The Field of Hastings* (1977).

19   Personal communication

20   Dunlop, J. 'The Story of the Rye road – Some Thoughts on Harold's Route' BDHS *Transactions* (1962–63).

21   In: Foord, K. and Clephane-Cameron, N. *1066 and the Battle of Hastings, Preludes, Events and Postscripts.* (2021).

22   Gillingham, JB. '1066 and warfare: the context and place (Senlac) of the Battle of Hastings' in Bates, D. (Ed.) *1066 in Perspective*, (2018).

23   Malfosse (OF) = Bad or evil ditch. See Clephane-Cameron, N. *The Malfosse Walk* (2nd Edition, 2020).

24   This is the Vegetian strategy, described in the 4th century by the Roman, Flavius Vegetius Renatus, which is discussed in more detail in 1066 and *The Battle of Hastings: Preludes, Events and Postscripts* and expounded in Gillingham, J. '"Up with Orthodoxy" – In Defence of Vegetian Warfare', *Journal of Medieval Military History* (2) (2004).

25   Shortbow and crossbow archers. It is believed that the longbow was not developed as a serious tactical anti-cavalry weapon in England until sometime around the reign of Edward I, and later in France, although it had been used by the Welsh and Scandinavians before that. The history of the longbow is, like most medieval developments, indefinite.

26   Possibly deployed by Conan I of Rennes against William in Brittany, whilst Harold was on campaign with William in 1064.

The manner of Harold's death is a perpetual mystery for historians.'

David Bates

If you can dream – and not make dreams your master

From 'If –' Rudyard Kipling

8
Harold, death, reality and mythology

The written record we have of the death of Harold Godwinson varies, as does the matter of the disposal of his body. David Bates comments 'The manner of Harold's death is a perpetual mystery for historians.' And there are unsubstantial claims that he survived the battle.

Although the probability that Harold died on the field of Hastings is extremely high, probably of the order of 99%, that other 1% of doubt has led to many myths. None of the many tales deny that he was either mortally or very seriously wounded to the point of near death, the latter allowing a glimpse of legend. None has ever claimed that he escaped on foot or horse without serious injury.

The first descriptive records within five years of the end of Harold's kingship were written by Norman, or Norman allied, clerics, therefore should be seen in that context.

The very first is the *Carmen de Hastingae Proelio*, written by Bishop Guy of Amiens,[1] the diocesan bishop of the County of Ponthieu, whose count, also named Guy, had done personal homage to William of Normandy, but with whom relations were tense. Both Guys had met Harold Godwinson in 1056, when Harold was undertaking some diplomatic duties on behalf of King Edward at Saint-Omer. The *Carmen* is a poem, that has much artistic and heroic licence, dated to before 1068 by Barlow, but it just might be later and derived from several sources. It is gorily graphic about Harold's death: He was lanced in the chest, beheaded, had his belly cut open with a spear, and a leg severed at the hip. He was certainly dead.

The *Carmen* then records a request after the battle from Harold's mother, Gytha, for her son's body, offering its weight in gold. William turned her down flat as 'inappropriate', but had the body parts gathered up, wrapped in purple linen, and taken back to his headquarters in Hastings. There he was to have him buried under a pile of stones on the seashore, but eventually allowed an earth burial, marked by a cairn on a Hastings cliff top; one local myth is that it is the mound on Black Horse Hill at Telham.[2] A cliff top grave will in time have almost certainly been lost to sea erosion since 1066.

The problem with the *Carmen* as a source is summed up those who have noted that when victory is seen as a divine reward, but conversely a punishment from God for the sins of losers, a fully evidence-based record of events will not be found with Bishop Guy of Amiens as its author.

Next is the *Gesta Normannorum Ducum* by William of Jumièges, written in 1070. He says no more than that Harold:

> 'fell covered with deadly wounds.

(i.e. more than one) and that at the dawn after the battle William

> 'despoiled the corpses of his enemies'.

This second phrase must refer to robbing the corpses of any usable or valuable items and weapons etc., rather than anything more heinous. There is nothing more specific. Collection of every item of potential further use from the dead and dying was the norm at that time. Weapons, armour, shields, leather goods etc. as well more personal items and things of value would be stripped from bodies and picked up from where they had been dropped or fallen, and at Hastings the Normans had probably over two weeks to do the searching. This accounts for why artefacts from medieval battles are hard to find and why the majority of ancient battlefields yield little to archaeologists. Organic matter rots and disappears and metal objects corrode away over the millennia, faster in some soils than others. This is well described by Curry and Foard,[3] even for battles 200–400 years and more after Hastings.

Then William of Poitiers, Duke William's chaplain, wrote his *Gesta Willelmi* 1071x1077. He has no description of the precise method of Harold's death but notes that the body was stripped of clothing and only recognised by 'certain signs', which suggests sufficient wounds, enough to cause recognition difficulties. There is no mention of who identified Harold. This story also repeats the refusal of the offer from his mother, Gytha, of Harold's weight in gold to release his body, as William 'deemed it unseemly' and he sardonically jested that Harold's body should be made 'guardian of sea and shore', which he had failed to be in life. The body was given to William Malet[4] to bury in a grave by the sea, with no indication of any location, although it cannot have been far from Hastings. The *Anglo-Saxon Chronicle (ASC)* written after 1066 by English clerics is minimalistic about the death of Harold in the 1066 entries –

> 'there king Harold was killed.' *(D version)*

and even more pithily

> 'there he fell' *(E version).*

Clearly the English authors of the *ASC* were convinced that Harold was dead, but they were saying no more, perhaps inhibited by circumstances from doing so.

The next record in time was the pictorial one of the *Bayeux Tapestry (BT),* probably sponsored by Odo of Bayeux/Kent, half-brother of William. The evidence points to it being designed and embroidered at Canterbury, by English embroiderers, but some have argued that it could have been with some involvement of Wilton Abbey and dowager Queen Edith. Some design elements clearly lean on late Anglo-Saxon manuscript illuminations. It was possibly installed at Bayeux for the cathedral's dedication in about 1077, at least by 1082 [+11 to +16 years],[5] when Odo fell from favour. Others have suggested that it may have been originally designed to be displayed in an early rectangular castle keep, possibly at Rochester or Dover in Odo's Kentish earldom, but it ended up in Bayeux.

The *Battle Tapestry*, the first panel of which is illustrated in figure 24, demonstrates the pervasiveness of the various stories about Harold's death into the modern world, and the lack of a universally accepted definite ending. It is not an old historical document but was produced as a community project in Battle town as part of the 950th commemoration of the Battle of Hastings in 2016. It imagines the battlefield at the end of the conflict, in the style of the *BT*, with a nod to several of the stories in one panel, including Edith and/or Gytha (with her gold in a little casket) finding Harold's body, the involvement of William Malet in Harold's burial, the multiple wounds and referencing Waltham Church.

Returning to the *BT* Harold dies in a scene marked HAROLD REX INTERFECTUS EST, of bloody confusion amid a sea of bodies, some missing heads, others already being stripped of arms and armour. Harold may be the figure grasping the shaft of an arrow, that may be in an eye, or the next figure falling backwards and dropping his axe, having been smitten with a heavy

Figure 24. The first panel of the *Battle Tapestry*.
© Tina Greene (Photo Peter Greene)

sword by a Norman horseman. It has been suggested that he has been represented twice, in a double scene, once with the arrow, then as he fell being hacked at, or even three times, the first representation being of him fighting next to his standard bearer. There are no follow up scenes in the *BT* to indicate what happened to his body.

The difficulty with the arrow story is that, according to Lewis and many others, the *BT* has had several restorations, additional and slightly longer arrows have appeared, and the tapestry had a restoration in this very area during the 19th century and is a little distorted (figures 25a and b). This raises the possibility of an alteration in direction of the 'arrow'. Note that the shaft of the 'arrow' is bent at the hand before the fletching – or alternatively a conversion from spear in the right hand into an arrow near an eye has been made – of which there is possible evidence from some stitching holes of a larger object on the reverse, well described by Bernstein.[6]

Charles Stothard[7] found embroidery stitching missing in 1818–19, particularly at the right-hand damaged end including around Harold's death and the end of battle scenes. He found fragments or traces of coloured thread or holes and where he knew the colour from the thread residues redrew these elements in that colour, making a pictorial 'repair', otherwise he drew in dotted lines. One of these dotted line features is the 'arrow'. The arrowhead end of this extends above the eye line to the brow band of Harold's helmet (figure 26). In 1872–74 Joseph Cundall made a full-scale photographic record of the *BT*.[8] Prints show the arrowhead in a lower position, slightly gapped from the 'O', pointing towards an eyebrow (figure 28). This difference has some significance as Stothard made some pictorial 'repairs'[9] and later physical repairs were based on his drawings. The Victoria and Albert Museum (V&A) in London holds copies of Cundall's work which can be viewed on request.

Earlier drawings from Benoît[10] of 1729 made into engravings by Montfaucon in about 1730 (figure 27) show the figure might have held a short spear, or javelin, there is certainly no fletching, although fletchings are shown on the arrows embedded in the shield. It may also be noted that comparing the drawing/engraving , photograph and tapestry that the 'O' of Harold in the text of this scene appears pushed upwards, is not partially or fully overlapped by the line of the arrow/spear as in Montfaucon's engravings or Stothard's drawings and is a little smaller.

Figure 25a. The critical section of the *BT*. *Bayeux Tapestry 11th Century ©Bayeux Museum.*

Figure 25b. This second image has been photographed and manipulated to exaggerate the finer features. Note the repair deformity above the helmet and the bent 'arrow', also slight displacement of the 'O' upwards when compared with the drawings of 1729–30 and 1818–19 below (figures 26 and 27), but agreeing with the later photographically derived image of 1873, made after repairs (figure 28). ©BBC from BBC News at bbc.co.uk/news https://www.bbc.co.uk/news/uk-44732897 (5 July 2018)

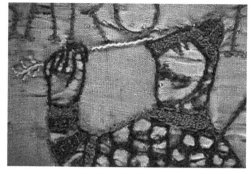

Figure 26. Extract from Stothard's drawing. Stothard's work is significant because it is a record from before repairs were carried out in the 19th century. Engraved by James Basire (1769–1822), after Stothard; hand-painted by Charles Alfred Stothard (1786-1821). The dotted lines represent lines of

stitching holes where there was no thread at Stothard's visits to Bayeux in 1818–19, and seem to end at the helmet band, well above the right eye, and is at a tangent to the 'O'. *A copy of the Stothard/Basire series of coloured engravings of the Bayeux Tapestry is in the Battle Museum of Local History collection.*

Figure 27. Magnification of same detail selection showing Harold's death in Montfaucon, B. de, 'Les Monumens de la Monarchie Françoise' Vol. 2 (1730), well before the French Revolution. The artist, Antoine Benoît, had strict instructions from Montfaucon to copy the tapestry 'faithfully', and his on-site drawings used grid lines for positional accuracy.

From the Collection numérisées de la bibliothèque de l'INHA, Open Licence

Figure 28. An extract from the full-size photograph made by Joseph Cundall and hand coloured by students from the School of Art, London in 1873, after 19th century repairs. The arrow fletchings appear as at present. *Image extract from https://www.bonhams.com*
An example of this may be viewed on request at the V&A. See https://collections.vam. ac.uk/item/O118318/bayeux-tapestry-photograph-cundall-co/bayeux-tapestry-photograph-cundall--co/

The *BT* has the first depiction of the 'arrow in the eye' story if it was so stitched by the embroiderers and the whole death of Harold scene is shown below (figure 29). The author is no expert on the Bayeux Tapestry but has some doubts about the arrow in the eye story. The reader may wish to decide for themselves if this was the original designer's intention or not after considering the information above and further numerous scholarly interpretations which can be found in the bibliography.[11]

Figure 29. The whole scene showing the killing of Harold (Frame 57).
Do we see three Harolds, first standing by the wyvern gonfalon bearer, wielding a spear, then with the 'arrow' (both have the same shield design) then dropping a battleaxe and falling backwards, hacked down by a Norman horseman? Also, two banner bearers – the second time left of the first, pierced by a spear and falling forwards with the deflated gonfalon trodden into the ground. Similarly in an earlier frame (51) Leofwine and Gyrth are each seen twice as they fall. *Bayeux Tapestry 11th Century ©Bayeux Museum*

It is possible that the earliest appearance in literary, as opposed to pictorial, sources came around the year 1080 when Amatus, a monk of Monte Cassino Abbey in

Italy, reported in his *L'Ystoire de li Normant (OF)* of Duke William's victory at Hastings after he had 'gouged out Harold's eye with an arrow'. A somewhat more vicious and gorier story than a chance injury. Marc Morris[12] points out that the only copy of this work is an interpolated 14th century French translation, which damages its credibility as a true source.

Baudri, Abbot of Bourgueil, in the poem he wrote for William the Conqueror's daughter, Adela, before 1102 *[+<36 years]* and who may have seen the BT, recounted how the battle came to an end after Harold had been fatally struck by an arrow, but fails to say exactly where he was struck. Henry of Huntingdon, who may not have seen the *BT*, in his *History of the English* first published in 1129 *[+63 years]* tells this same story.

No written account of this incident was firsthand, all are 35 years or more after the battle. Other accounts start to appear a few years after this time. *John of Worcester* in his compilation in about 1118 *[+52 years]* of earlier material says, without details, for 1066:

> 'About twilight the king alas fell'.

The *Gesta Regum Anglorum* of William of Malmesbury from about 1125 *[+59 years]* says:

> '...when his brain was pierced by an arrow and he fell, the English fled without respite till the night....One of the knights hacked at his thigh with a sword as he lay on the ground'.

Historia Anglorum of Henry of Huntington, about 1130 *[+64 years]* says:

> 'The arrows fell around King Harold, and he ...was... struck in the eye'.

and in *The Ecclesiastical History of England and Normandy* by Ordericus Vitalis, who was born in Atcham, Shropshire, England in 1074 but became a monk in Saint-Évroult, Normandy when aged ten, and may have started writing in 1110x15. He died 1141x42 aged 67 plus, we find *[minimum +44 years, almost certainly more]*:

> 'Harold could not be found at first but was recognized by other 'tokens'. The corpse was borne to the duke's camp and delivered to William Mallet for interment near the seashore, 'which had long been guarded by his arms''.

Benoît de Sainte-Maure wrote his *Chronique des ducs de Normandie* in about 1175 *[+109 years]* and repeats that:

> 'Harold was buried at Hastings, that his mother offered money that was rejected, as there was no wish to give the body back, and that William Malet, neither youth nor vassal, was assigned the burial task.'

Sources for all the above later texts must have been *Carmen de Triumpho Normannico, Gesta Normannorum Ducum, Gesta Willelmi* and perhaps the *Bayeux Tapestry*, plus perhaps some unknown lost informants. We are now 50–100 years plus away from the event and put into context this is akin to a monk with no or at best second-hand military knowledge, writing about World War I without the benefit of detailed records, photographs and movies, from a few limited written sources written by army chaplains plus second-hand oral histories.

Poitiers' *Gesta Willelmi* was the main source for the first part of the *Chronicle of Battle Abbey (CBA)*, written after 1155 *[+>89 years]*, and maybe also using as a secondary source an early version of Wace's *Roman de Rou* – as a 12th century manuscript of this was once in the Battle Abbey library.[13] The *CBA* itself woefully understates the event with:

> When their king was laid low by a chance blow....

To this point all the records indicate a death on the battlefield, with the later scribes picking up their information from the earlier tales. Later in the 12th century we start to pick up on rumours and survival myths.

Wace, was born on Jersey between 1090 and 1110, and went to Caen as a small child. Writing the *Roman de Rou* from about 1155 until about mid-1170 *[+89 to 104 years]*, he records;

> ....Then it chanc'd that an arrow which fell from on high, smote Harold the king, – and put out his right eye, in his agony wrenching the point from the wound, He broke short the shaft, – which he dashed to the ground...

Later he says;

> «Li reis Herant en fu portez, a Waichan, fu enterrez, Mais jo ne sai qui le uporta, Ne jo ne sai qui l'enterra.» (OF)

> *'King Harold was taken away and buried at Waltham, but I do not know who took him. Nor do I know who buried him.'*

This is the first mention of Waltham, and we do not know his source. Even so the record remains that the king was clearly dead when taken there. Wace often follows William of Poitiers, but is known to diverge, and here there is a divergence, even though he admits he does not know the details. Wace was finishing writing at the time the *Chronicle of Waltham Abbey*(CWA) started to be scribed at Waltham Abbey in Essex by an anonymous canon who entered the college church there aged five. It was written after the college was replaced by a new Augustinian abbey in 1177 *[+> 111 years]*.

Harold had been a huge benefactor at Waltham, including rebuilding its church of the Holy Cross in 1060 and granting it 70 hides of land. Not only that but he gave it a large collection of Holy relics, expensive vestments and silver and gold ornamentations. He stopped to pray there on his way back to London from Stamford Bridge in 1066.

The *CWA* has two named monks from Waltham, Osegode Cnoppe and Ailric Childemaister, who accompanied Harold on his march to the south coast fearing that their patron would be killed in battle. Their fears became reality and Osegode and Ailric sought permission to seek for Harold's body, and to take it to Waltham for interment. They had a long and fruitless search, and Osegode went back to Waltham with this news. The canons advised him to take Harold's concubine, Edith Swanneshals (or Edith Swan-neck), back to the battle site.[14] She then recognized Harold's body by secret marks which were known only to herself. This event is imagined by a sculpture at Hastings (figure 30).

A local myth in Battle holds that Edith watched the battle from the 'Watch Oak', a rise just north of Battle town, west of Caldbec Hill. It is a good story, but the area was not called the 'Watch Oak' until the 14th century. If she had been nearby it would have saved the Waltham monks a long journey …

The *CWA* story continues with Osegode placing the body on a bier and carrying it in solemn procession to 'Battle Bridge' (unknown location, possibly an area near Redhill in Surrey, or a Thames crossing), where it was met by the whole brotherhood of Waltham. They took the corpse to Waltham and buried it in the choir of the then abbey church.

**Figure 30. Marble sculpture at Grosvenor Gardens, St. Leonards on Sea of
'Edith finding the body of Harold on the battlefield of Hastings'**
*It expresses the imagined moment after the Battle of Hastings in 1066 when the mortally wounded King
Harold II, the last Anglo-Saxon King of England, was found by his partner of 20 years.*[15,16] Photo: Keith Foord

There have been many physical changes over the years around the abbey at Waltham. Harold's abbey church was replaced by a new Norman church on a slightly different site and the author of the *CWA* claims to have witnessed the moving of Harold's body at that time. stating that it happened within the period of the scribe's residence in Waltham Abbey (1124–1177). The body, which was claimed to be Harold's, was moved no less than three times, due to more building work in the church and in 1538x1539 the abbey church was three-quarters destroyed at the Dissolution. The townspeople claimed it as their parish church, so its nave was spared for that purpose, to remain more or less as it is today. This was unlike at Battle where sadly the great abbey church was completely destroyed in 1538 as there was already an adequate parish church (St. Mary's).

The Scots philosopher and historian David Hume wrote in 1754x1762 that Harold had been buried by the high altar of the Norman church and later his remains had been moved to the choir of the later Augustinian abbey. This position would lie outside the extent of the post-Dissolution church. Visitors at that time of his visit were shown a stone slab bearing the inscription:

> Hic iacet Haroldus infelix (L)
> *"Here lies Harold the unfortunate".*

Daniel Defoe's earlier *A tour thro' the whole island of Great Britain (1724–7)* records for Waltham:

> No monument was, as I can find, built for him, only a flat grave-stone, on which was engraven, *Harold Infoelix*[17]

This slab has since disappeared. The site of the Augustinian abbey high altar is marked today by a small square stone pillar inscribed:

> Harold King of England, Obit 1066

and a slab with the words:

> This stone marks the position of the high altar behind which King Harold is said to have been buried 1066.

The same geological survey company which successfully helped locate the remains of King Richard III in 2012 in Leicester carried out privately funded scanning at Waltham Abbey in 2014. A report was made of an unmarked grave close to an old wall, but this has gone no further and permission to open the grave was denied.

Winters wrote a review in 1877 that describes notes and findings about coffins, skeletons and various pieces of funereal masonry found at Waltham in the 17th and 18th centuries. Various findings have also been described by Beattie. Most of the objects appear to have been lost into curious and acquisitive private hands

Figure 31. The approximate site of the possible burial of Harold, marking the estimated site of the demolished Augustinian Abbey's high altar

way before the time of supervised archaeology. Accounting for this souvenir hunting and given the extent of multiple rebuilds and body moving on this site the chances of finding anything of Haroldian historical value must be slim indeed. More recent archaeological work on the church sites, undertaken between 1984–1991, was reported by Huggins et al.

The stories get wilder. The *Vita Haraldii* is the first part of the *Codex ruber* or *Waltham Abbey miscellany*. A version of this dated after 1345 is held in the British Library (*Harley MS 3776*). This first part is recognised as a copy of an earlier lost document. The first translator from MS 3776 of the *Vita Haraldii*, Walter de Gray Birch (1842–1924), who worked in the Department of Manuscripts at the British Museum from 1864 to 1902 and published extensively on Anglo-Saxon studies, thought that from its literary structure that it could have been first written about 150 years after 1066 (i.e., about 1220). Matthews who looks in detail at the content of the whole work finds some conflicts between the *Vita* and the overall *Chronicle* but concurs that the first version of the *Vita* was scribed in the early 13th century.

Summarised the Vita Haraldii says:

> Edith had mistaken another corpse for Harold. Harold had been found still breathing by four Saxon women who did not realise who it was. They carried him away from the spot, and he was recognized by two men, who took him to Winchester, where he remained hidden for two years and was cured by a Saracen woman . After that, he went to 'Saxony', hoping to recruit 'Saxons and Norwegians' to assist him in regaining England from the Normans. He failed and in several dream sequences passed the rest of his days in retirement, first visiting Rome. He returned in disguise, under

the name of Christian, to England, and lived ten years as a hermit, in the neighbourhood of Dover. He had an anchorite servant called Sebricht. He then went to the Welsh borders where he experienced insults from the Welsh, and finally went to Chester, dying at an old age in a little cell attached to the church of St. John, confessing on his deathbed that he was King Harold.

The online blog of 'The Clerk of Oxford' comments:

> The *Vita Haraldii* is somewhat akin to modern counterfactual history, a thought experiment which explores one of history's perpetual 'what ifs'; as with many medieval historical texts, to take it too literally is to underestimate its complexity.

These stories were repeated in several old Chronicles – including *Brompton's, Knyghton's, Aelred of Rievaulx'* and *Giraldus Cambrensis'* (*Gerald the Welshman*) *Chronicles*. The *Brompton Chronicle* written between 1425–50 says, without any preamble:

> He went to live around Chester in a secret place and lived a holy life. It was believed to be in a solitary cell near the church. Here he made a final confession. His tomb is in St Johns Church. Some say that King Henry I when returning via Chester had a conversation with him.

But he also covered the options by additionally saying (author's poor translation):

> I say, that because many doubted this custom, and sensing the profoundness of the matter, that, as accepted, Harold's head injury from arrows caused his death. She (? Gytha) contemptuously arranged that his body was sent as a penance by William to, and accepted by, Waltham and buried in the same church in honour of the holy cross that he (Harold) had installed there.

But Gerald of Wales liked a good story. When writing of Chester in his *The Itinerary of Archbishop Baldwin*[18] *through Wales in 1188* he says:

> It is also asserted, that the remains of Harold are here deposited. He was the last of the Saxon kings in England, and as a punishment for his perjury, was defeated in the Battle of Hastings, fought against the Normans. Having received many wounds and lost his left eye[19] by an arrow in that engagement, he is said to have escaped to these parts, where, in holy conversation, leading the life of an anchorite, and being a constant attendant at one of the churches of this city, he is believed to have terminated his days happily. The truth of these two circumstances

was declared (and not before known) by the dying confession of each party.

The various versions of *Haralds Saga* all agree that Harold was killed at Hastings, but Harold's apparent survival is surprisingly otherwise well recorded in heroic Scandinavian sources. In the 14th century Icelandic saga of Edward the Confessor, *Saga Játvarðar konungs hins helga*, the writer supplemented his material on the king with history, anecdote, and legend on various topics.

This includes:

> Some friends of king Harold fared to the battlefield and looked for his body, and found him alive, and bore him off to be healed; he was cured in secret. And when he was made whole, his friends offered to make war on William, and get the land whatever it cost. But king Harold would not do that, stating he understood that God would not grant him the realm. And perhaps it is better so. Then the king undertook a better plan to give up this world's honour and went into a cell and was a hermit while he lived, so serving Almighty God unceasingly both night and day.

The final chapter of this also contains an account of a post-Conquest Anglo-Saxon emigration to Byzantium[20] led by one 'Earl Sigurðr' (?Siward) of Gloucester. The reason for noting this here is that an earlier, but confused, account of this is given by Ordericus Vitalis (b. 1075), written in the first half of the twelfth century, and a more detailed narrative was included in the *Chronicon universale anonymi Laudunensis*, written in Latin by an English monk in the monastery of Saint Martin at Laon in the early 13th century. So, the sources for the *Saga Játvarðar* cannot be entirely ignored, although sagas are sometimes regarded as somewhat suspect sources as they originate as mainly oral histories, subject to distortion and heroic embellishments.

From the end of another fourteenth-century Icelandic text called *Hemings þáttr Áslákssonar*, is the story of a (fictional) Norwegian named Heming who serves King Edward, then Harold II and becomes involved in the English battles of Stamford Bridge and Hastings, we get this (much abbreviated) story:

> On the night after the battle two locals went foraging on the battlefield. They saw a light over one pile of bodies and found a severely wounded man. This was Harold. They took him home and hid him from William's men. They then asked for help from a Norwegian man called Heming. The next day Heming met Harold and suggested that he could soon win back England. Harold said that would be forcing men to break their oaths to William and that he would follow the example of the defeated King Olaf Tryggvason, who went to Greece and served God. He would take to a hermit's cell in Canterbury and live only on food brought to him by Heming. He was there for three years and saw only Heming and a priest

who confessed him. He became ill and died. The bells were tolled, and King William asked why. Heming told him that it was because Harold Godwinson had died. William went to see the body threatening to kill Heming if it were true, but when he confirmed that it was Harold, he changed his mind about Heming and offered him a place as one of his own bodyguards, but if he did not want to do that he would give him three pounds a year. Heming refused both offers and said that he wished to live as a hermit in Harold's old cell. William buried Harold with honours, and Heming went off to live in the cell, where he eventually died. And there is no more to tell of Heming.

And it all still goes on... Edward, Lord Lytton's historical romance, *Harold: The Last of the Saxon Kings*[21] was written in 1848 with the author's aim 'to solve the problem of how to produce the greatest amount of dramatic effect at the least expense of historical truth' and Lord Tennyson wrote a play; *Harold, a drama* published in 1877.[22] At the end of the play Edith Swan-neck drops down dead by Harold's body and they are buried together. Rudyard Kipling wrote a short story, *The Tree of Justice*, a rather rambling tale, included in his 1910 collection, *Rewards and Fairies*,[23] a sequel to *Puck of Pook's Hill,* where an old King Harold (who had survived Hastings) meets King Henry I and finally dies in the arms of a Saxon knight. The romance, this story and Tennyson's play are all pure historical fantasy fiction, but show that the legends, as they say, still have legs.

An outlying and very readable book is *The Golden Warrior* written by Hope Muntz (1907–1981) in 1948 (figure 32). It is fiction but its background is scholarly and followed the non-fiction history that seemed most probable. In the epilogue she ventured into a 'Walthamist' totally fictional story of Edith finding Harold dead on the battlefield, but ventures no further into mythology. The book is out of print, but copies can be found. She was Canadian by birth but was raised in southern England. Later she became a Fellow of both the Society of Antiquaries and the Royal Historical Society, and co-editor of the Oxford Mediaeval Texts translation of the *Carmen* published in 1972. She was one of the first Vice-Presidents of BDHS in 1951 and remained so until 1959. In 1966 she scripted a documentary film *The Norman Conquest in the Bayeux Tapestry* which featured Edith Evans, Anthony Quayle and Robert Hardy and was produced by Talking Pictures. This is listed by the BFI, but unfortunately they do not have a copy of

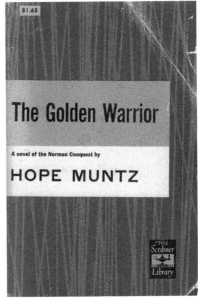

Figure 32. The author's slightly battered 1949 copy of *The Golden Warrior*

the film.[24.25] Also, in 1966 she produced a 64-page book covering the three battles of 1066, *Battle for the Crown,* which may have been what is now called a 'tie in' with the film. In later life she lived in Dorset with her sister, Elizabeth, a sculptor, whose statue of Harold had been installed against the SW buttress of Waltham Abbey Church in 1964. Between 1974 and her death she was the Honorary President of BDHS.

In 1954 bones with its skull and part of its leg were found in a stone sarcophagus at Holy Trinity Church, Bosham in West Sussex. The subsequent coroner's report, (and it should be remembered that at that time there was no modern DNA etc. sampling available) suggested that the adult bones were of someone older than Harold at his death. There was renewed interest from about 1994 led by John Pollock (d.2010) a local resident who was convinced that these were the remains of King Harold II and wrote both a play and a book about Harold.[26.27] This led to a request in 2003 to exhume the grave, which was refused by the Chancellor of the Diocese of Chichester in a detailed judgement.[28] The church also contains the remains of a child who possibly drowned nearby, reputedly a young daughter of King Cnut.[29] Therefore, there has been no recent possibility to obtain DNA from the known skeletons.

What can we conclude from all this?

1. The early stories all confirm, or do not deny, that Harold died at Hastings from multiple wounds which may include an arrow in the eye. He may have been buried on a Hastings cliff top; in which case if undisturbed the grave will have been lost to the sea by erosion over the centuries, a process by which much of the original Hastings' history has sadly disappeared.

2. The body may have been removed to Waltham sometime after first burial. David Bates suggests that this a solution which would have been 'least unusual'. But it has also been argued that William may not have wanted anything left at all to become an Haroldian shrine.

3. The stories about a burial at Waltham do not appear until the mid-12th century, over 100 years later. A cult did indeed develop which was apparently embarrassing for the abbey under early Norman rule, but did not stop it over a century later in 1184 from achieving royal peculiar status from Henry I, similar to the status of Battle Abbey as given by William I. His body could have been exhumed from its site at Hastings later, and taken to Waltham, but there has been so much disturbance at the Waltham site, with multiple abbey and church rebuilding, body moving, and souvenir robbing that the chance of finding anything there is very remote.

4. Stories of Harold's unlikely survival, half dead, take on auras of mythology, but refuse to go away. They have features of conspiracy theories, and have suffered from multiple repetitions in old chronicles, sagas and romantic prose poems of varying repute, new variations appearing even centuries after the events.

5. Yet again, we have stories arising from the Battle of Hastings and Harold's death that because of an absence of absolute proof will not go away and will almost certainly never be fully elucidated. The stories have partly contributed over the years to varying views in Britain on how to perceive the effects of Norman Conquest after Harold's defeat, which is explored in Part 2 of this book.

Notes

1   Guy was a son of Enguerrand I of Ponthieu, but bishop of the French diocese of Amiens. His nephew also called Guy was the Count of Ponthieu encountered by Harold and another nephew Hugh was probably the Hugh involved in the slaying of Harold at Hastings.

2   Clearly not a cliff top, although a high point on the Battle ridge.

3   Curry, A. and Foard, G. 'Where are the dead of medieval battles? A preliminary survey' *Journal of Conflict Archaeology* 11, 2–3 (2016).

4   William Malet is believed to have had some part English ancestry, possibly distantly related to Earl Leofric of Mercia.

5   From this point forwards the elapsed time in years after 1066 of the dating of records/ scripts is emphasised by dark red text in brackets

6   In: Bernstein, D. *The Mystery of the Bayeux Tapestry* (1986)

7   Stothard wrote about his visits to Bayeux, the condition that he found the BT to be in, including damaged areas, which he lightly drew in on his copy. Stothard, CA. 'Some Observations on the Bayeux Tapestry', *Archaeologia* 19 (1821) copied in Gameson, R. (Ed.) *The study of the Bayeux Tapestry* (1997)

8   Over a two-month period in 1872, on 186 full sized glass plates still in possession of the V&A. Only six full-size copies of the BT were made on paper in 1874, using a technique called the Woodbury process. Two copies are held by the V&A. The South Kensington Museum, now the V&A, gave two copies to Bayeux. The full-sized copy sent to Bayeux has been lost, but they do still have a half scale one. One was sold by Bonhams in a sale of the Michael Bennett-Levy Collection in 2009 for £6000. Copies were hand coloured by students of the now Royal College of Arts and a copy was made available to the 'Ladies of Leek' at the Leek School of Art in 1885 – 86 to make an accurate full-sized embroidery copy, "so that England should have a copy of its own", which can now be seen at Reading Museum. Quaintly they censored any human genitalia in true prudish Victorian style, adding underpants, so it wasn't quite a true copy...

9   The author on first reading his words in *Archaeologia* thought that he had made physical repairs!

10   Antoine Benoît, had strict instructions from Montfaucon to copy the tapestry 'faithfully'. Benoît's original drawings used grid lines for positional accuracy.

11   The secondary sources are truly numerous. Books and papers by Bates, Bernstein, Foys, Gameson, Hicks, Lemagnen, Lewis, Musgrove, Owen-Crocker, Stothard, Thorpe and Wilson are all listed in the biography but there are many other publications, which shows how perplexing and alluring the story is to historians.

12   Morris, M. *The Norman Conquest* (2013) p.186

13   This copy is now at the British Library (Royal MS 4 C.xi), 'Liber Abbatria Sancti Martini de Bello' is written in one of the folios.

14   The author can only comment that in the time that must have been taken to go the

67 miles (108 km) back and forth to Waltham Abbey that the battlefield, strewn with English corpses, must have deteriorated to be a grim place to search for a loved one.

15   Made by the sculptor Charles Wilke in 1875 for Lord Brassey, the town's then MP, the statue spent its first decades indoors, first in the Brassey Institute and then Hastings Museum, but was moved onto the museum lawn in the 1930s and again to its current location in the 1950s.

16   The statue is in a poor state and has lost its fine detail. Clearly it should never have been displayed outdoors. It needs restoration, and to be moved to an indoor display if possible. A group has been formed to raise awareness of its condition, see: https://friendsofedith.org.uk/

17   With a 30-year gap, and the slight word and spelling differences were these even the same slabs?

18   Archbishop Baldwin of Forde, Archbishop of Canterbury between 1185–1190. The monks of Christ Church Priory opposed his appointment, and this involved Abbot Odo of Battle (see: Foord, K. *Conquest to Dissolution 1067–1538* (2019))

19   Clearly an error if the *BT* is correct, it was the right eye if any.

20   Shepard, J. 'The English and Byzantium: A Study of their role in the Byzantine Army in the later Eleventh Century'. *Traditio* ((1973), 29, 53–92.

21   An e-copy can be found via Project Gutenberg. Lytton was a prolific writer.

22   Critics were damning and it was considered unperformable. A world first performance is claimed by Yale University Dramatic Association in June 1915. See Eidson, JO. *The New England Quarterly* Vol. 37, No. 3 (1964), pp. 387–390. The Irish author F Frankfort Moore significantly adapted it in 1926 and the play was performed retitled *1066* at the former Palace Pier Pavilion at St Leonards-on-Sea on 14,15 and 16 October that year. It generated a considerable correspondence in the local newspaper and a request was made for the transcript to be translated to French for a performance at Rouen (Doherty, G. *Personal communication*). In 1928 it was performed by the Birmingham Repertory Company and at the Court Theatre, London, 2–24 April for 25 apathetically received performances, noted only as Laurence Olivier's first major performance in London playing Harold. (See: Trewin, JC. *We'll hear a Play* (1949)). If this was the original play it would have been the first unadapted performance in the UK.

23   *Rewards and Fairies* also contains 'If–' , perhaps one of the most famous and popular poems in English.

24   See http://collections-search.bfi.org.uk/web/Details/ChoiceFilmWorks/
150059428

25   No connection is known between these producers and the modern TV company of the same name.

26   Mme Sylvette Lemagnen is thanked for this information.

27   See: Pollock, J. *A play in verse and prose animating eight panels from the Bayeux Tapestry* (1994) and Pollock, J. *Is King Harold II buried in Bosham Church* (1996).

28   http://www.bosham.org/bosham-magazine/history/King-Harold-remains.html; In the Consistory Court of the Diocese of Chichester CH 79/03 24 November 2003–10 December 2003 Re Holy Trinity, Bosham.

29   Cnut's dally with the tides is also believed to have been at Bosham.

A garden here – May breath and bloom of spring –
The cuckoo yonder from an English elm
Crying 'with my false egg I overwhelm
The native nest:' and fancy hears the ring
Of harness, and that dreadful arrow sing,
And Saxon battleaxe clang on Norman helm.
Here rose the dragon-banner of our realm:
Here fought, here fell, our Norman-slander'd king,
O Garden blossoming out of English blood!
O strange hate-healer Time! We stroll and stare
Where might made right eight hundred years ago;
Might, right? Ay good, so all things make for good –
But he and he, if soul and soul, are where
Each stands full face with all he did below.

Show-day at Battle Abbey 1876,
Alfred, Lord Tennyson

9

Harold's Family after his Death

After 14 October 1066 Harold had a surviving parent, two surviving wives, three surviving sisters – one of which was Edward the Confessor's Queen Edith, a surviving brother, Wulfnoth, and a number of surviving offspring, female, who could create dynastic issues for the Normans if they had children, and male, who could do the same and cause military mischief. There was a stepdaughter and some nephews and nieces. Much here is prompted by Barlow's *The Godwins* but is added to by significant new interpretations and scholarship which has become available since 2002.

Harold's mother **Gytha Thorkelsdóttir** was clearly still alive at the time of his death. If Harold was born in 1022x1026 she must have been at least 60 years old at that time. Eight of her known children were still alive at the beginning of 1066, Sweyn had died on a pilgrimage and Alfgar, if he existed, had probably died in his 20s. But she had almost certainly had even more pregnancies. At the end of 1066 she had lost four sons, Tostig, killed at Stamford Bridge and Harold, Gyrth and Leofwine, all killed at Hastings. Wulfnoth was still languishing in Normandy as a hostage, awaiting his fate, which we shall find out below. Her daughters, Gunnhild, Aelfgifu, and Edith are soon to be discussed, in that order

As has been previously noted she was Danish, sister-in-law to Cnut, and sister of two Danish jarls. She would have been well educated and her children and grandchildren would have received a fine education for the times. As an indication of this, we are told by Godfrey of Cambrai, a Prior of Winchester between 1082 and 1104, that Harold's sister, Queen Edith, knew astronomy and mathematics and was also something of a linguist, certainly speaking Irish. All the Godwin offspring were:

Educated in those arts that would make them useful to future rulers.

After the Battle of Hastings, Gytha Thorkelsdóttir, with her daughter **Gunnhild Godwinsdotter,** Harold's sister, had taken refuge in a house in Exeter that belonged to the Earls of Wessex. The city was determined to resist the Conqueror. Whilst William returned to Normandy in 1067, the city was further fortified. After William returned his siege of Exeter, probably in January/February 1068, lasted about 18 days. When the city capitulated it was spared sacking. After this, William went on into Cornwall, but was back in Winchester by 23 March. Whether King Harold's sons by Edith Swanneck, Godwin, Edmund and Magnus, were also present is not recorded, they may have been rebelling near York. Gytha escaped with Gunnhilda by the city's water gate and down the river Exe before the surrender, then travelled north overland to a north coast port, or sailed around Land's End to the island of Flatholm in the Bristol Channel, from where she finally sought refuge with Count Baldwin VI of Flanders. The *ASC(D)* says:

> 1067 'And Gytha, Harold's mother, and many distinguished men's wives with her, went out to Flatholme and stayed there for some time and so went from there overseas to Saint-Omer.'

Gytha entered the nunnery at Saint-Omer, where she died in about 1070. Gunnhild lived in Bruges for some 20 years but sometime visited Denmark. She died in Bruges on 24 August 1087. For the kindness she had received at the hands of its burghers, it is said that she bequeathed her jewels to their Collegiate Church — jewels said to be so precious that, when they were sold a century later, a sufficient sum was realized to pay for the church's restoration.[1] She was laid to rest in the cloister of Saint Donatien. Her life history (with nothing about the jewels) was confirmed in Latin on a lead plaque (figure 33) found when her tomb was opened in

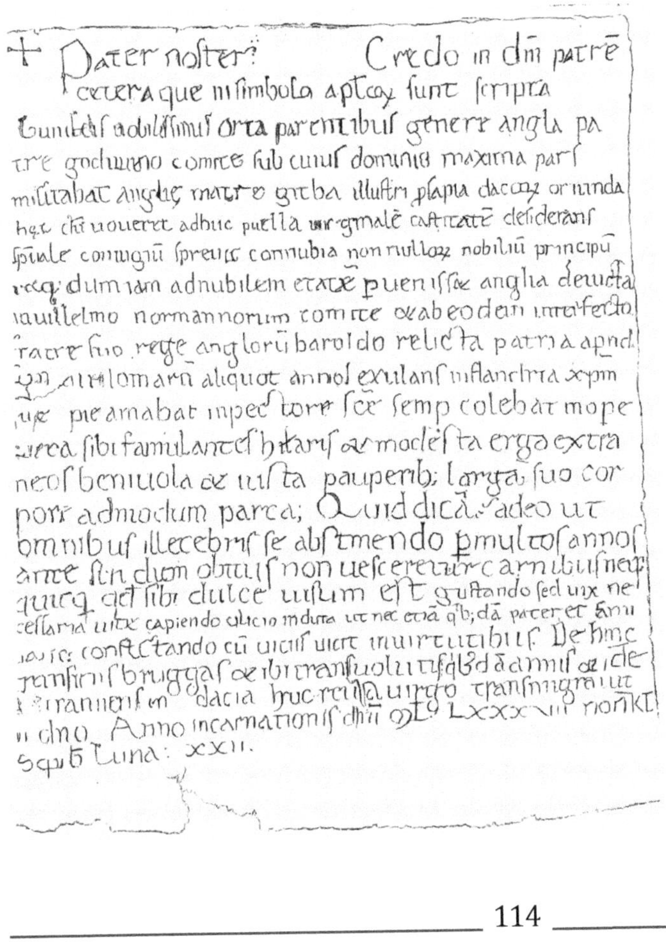

Figure 33. A facsimile of the plate from: 'Observations on the Coffin-Plate and History of Gunilda, sister of the Saxon King Harold II.' by G. F. Beltz, Esq. F.S.A., Lancaster Herald, in a Letter to Sir Henry Ellis, K.H. F.R.S. Secretary (1833) from *Archaeologia*, Volume 25 via Google books

1786 after which she was reburied, with the plaque. But Saint Donatien church was destroyed only 13 years later in 1799 during the French Revolution. Fortunately, the plaque was found again in 1804 when what was left of the church was demolished. It can still be seen in the museum at Saint Saviour's Cathedral[2] in Bruges.

Wulfnoth, Harold's youngest brother, who had been held hostage by William since 1052, after being sent to Normandy by King Edward the Confessor against the good behaviour of the Godwins after their revolt of 1051, was now very vulnerable. Harold had tried to free him in 1064 and maybe in 1056, but William had retained him as hostage against Harold's good faith in whatever deal he and Harold may have made.

Wulfnoth did survive through the Conquest, still in custody in Normandy. He was fated to remain in Normandy until after William's death in 1087, when he was briefly released and returned to England with King William (Rufus) II. He was then re-confined at Winchester in relatively comfortable circumstances and died in 1094 at Salisbury. He appears to have been 'let out' occasionally to sign charters of William II, including one at Hastings in January 1091 concerning Bishop Osmund's re-organisation at Salisbury Cathedral. It is not clear why he was there, except to wonder if it was still considered too dangerous to leave a Godwinson in England whilst the King fought in Normandy. In early 1091 Rufus was en route to Normandy to confront his brother, Robert Curthose.

Ælfgifu Godwinsdotter, believed born about 1035, sister of Harold, is a bit of a mystery. She is listed as Ælfgifu (Ælviva), Abbess of Wilton 1065–1067 by Knowles et al.[3] and is also recorded elsewhere as 'Ælfgyva' or 'Alfyne'.[4] She is listed in *PASE Domesday* as 'Ælfgifu 29, abbess of Wilton', holding lands worth £298.54 and lord of lands worth £13.15 in 1066. Wilton Abbey held two manors in the Rape of Hastings – one in the north of Hailesaltede hundred[5] worth £2.13 the other in Henhurst hundred worth 25 pence, both probably gifted by King Edward via Queen Edith.

She was probably the sister who was being offered as wife to one of William's magnates as part of the deal Harold and William may have been hatching in Normandy. In return, Harold would have formally married a daughter of William's, probably Adeliza/Adela. The marriage deals were blown out of the water when Harold took the English throne and formally married Ealdgyth of Mercia.

See the 'Ælfgyva' scene in the *BT* described above. The architecture depicted in that enigmatic scene with its sexual inuendo is different from the rest of the Tapestry, and it has been suggested that it represented Wilton Abbey rather than somewhere in Normandy. Some have suggested that Wilton and not Canterbury was the site of the embroidering of the *BT*, or there may have been some involvement of embroiders from Wilton, and this puzzling insertion does raise a question mark.

The last abbess of Wilton surrendered the convent to the commissioners of King Henry VIII on 25 March 1539 at the Dissolution of the Monasteries. Regrettably, nothing remains of the stone abbey that Queen Edith had rebuilt at Wilton which was consecrated in 1065. Wilton House occupies its site and there are no ancient ruins left after Henry VIII's vandalism and later building on the same site to give us any architectural evidence .

The two wives of Harold have little record after 1066. The first was **Ealdgyth Swann hnesce** (*Ealdgyth Swannesshals / Edith Swan-necked / Edith Gentle-swan*) a daughter of a prominent, but not definitely identified, family in East Anglia. It has been proposed that she was the so called 'Edith the Fair' identified as a very wealthy woman 'in the time of King Edward' in *Domesday*[6] She is also identified as Eddeva pulcra.[7] It would make sense, given that she was a Godwin by marriage and that they were great property acquisitors, but it is not absolutely proven and there were many other Ediths, with varying spellings.

To all effects she disappears post-Conquest[8] with her lands usurped by various Normans, but mainly by the Breton, Ralf de Gaël, who became Earl of Norfolk (also see the synopsis of her daughter Gunnhild Haroldsdotter below). He in turn lost them to Count Alan Rufus in 1075 after revolting against William in Brittany.

Harold and she had probably married 'in the Danish way' when Harold became Earl of East Anglia, and he was with her for over 20 years. They had a number of children, Godwin, Edmund, Magnus, probably Ulf (see below), Gytha and Gunnhild. There is a great deal of romantic fiction about Edith Swan-neck which generates the usual confusion of ideas and reality.

Harold had only formally married his second wife, **Ealdgyth of Mercia**,[9] the daughter of the late Earl Aelfgar of Mercia and widow of Welsh King Gruffydd ap Llewelyn, early in 1066 after becoming king, to cement his relationship with her brothers, Earls Edwin of Mercia and Morcar of Northumbria. Such was the fate of daughters and sisters of earls to be used as political pawns. They are recorded as maybe having had two sons, **Harold Haroldson** and **Ulf**, but it is much more likely that Ulf was Edith Swan-neck's last son, possibly a teenager in 1066.

Harold's new brother-in-laws, Edwin and Morcar,[10] had sent their sister to Chester for safety at the time of the invasion. There she gave birth to little Harold Haroldson. Ealdgyth and Harold junior were able to flee to Ireland sometime in 1070. The future of Ealdgyth is uncertain. One highly dubious claim is that she died at Rhuddlan Castle in Wales in 1086. Another is that she was still alive in England at *Domesday*. It is possible that she ended up at the Abbey of La Chaise-Dieu in the Auvergne, France, where an English 'Queen Edith' might have sought a cure for leprosy. This interesting speculation is based on a surviving fragment of a customary from La Chaise-Dieu which became local lore in France and is discussed by both Baxter and Beech.[11,12,13] Gaussin[14] also reviews this and cites the opening line of a hymn sung for Queen Edith at the abbey which is noted as a hymn in Latin for her soul on All Souls Day.[15,16]

Quaesumus, Domine, ora pro regina Angliae famula tua Editha..., (L)
[*Lord, we earnestly ask for the Queen of England, your handmaiden Edith...*]

But this almost certainly refers to Edith Godwinsdotter as quoted by Gardon[17] in an early 17th century history, where an 'Edith' funds a dormitory in thanks for a cure for leprosy from

the skills and prayers of St Adelelm'.

What we can be sure about is that Edith Godwinsdotter is buried at Westminster, not in the Auvergne, so maybe there really are the remains of Ealdgyth of Mercia in the monumental tomb at La Chaise-Dieu. If so, and she was ministered to by Adelelm, she must gone there before 1078.[18] It was probable that Adelelm's curative skills were well known as later Queen Matilda would seek his help for a lesser affliction.[19] Did Edith somehow advise Ealdgyth to go there or were his powers general knowledge amongst the nobility?

Ealdgyth had had at least one daughter by her first husband, **Nest or Nesta, Harold's stepdaughter** who would later marry Osbern fitzRichard.[20] After the Conquest, Osbern had gained manors across the Midlands, south of Birmingham and Coventry.

There were also two sons by Gruffydd: Ithel, who was killed at and Maredudd who died soon after, the Welsh internecine Battle of Mechain[21] in 1067x69. These must have been half-brothers of Nesta, from Gruffydd's previous marriage, as, if Ealdgyth had been their mother, they could only have been aged 10 or so at that time. There is no record that Harold had ever had any interaction with his stepdaughter nor his wife's stepsons.

Ulf Haroldson appears to have fallen into the hands of William during the post-1066 confusions and was imprisoned by him in Normandy. As with his uncle Wulfnoth, he was freed on the death of William in 1087 but, in his case, he passed into the hands of Robert Curthose, who released him at the same time as Duncan, the son of Malcolm III of Scotland after knighting them both. Duncan briefly joined William II Rufus in England then went on to dispute the crown of Scotland with Donald III Bane, and was crowned as Duncan II but then murdered after six to seven months, when Donald regained the throne. Barlow suggested that Ulf could have joined Duncan, others have proposed that he went on crusade with Robert, but whatever happened he was not recorded again.

It is probable that later in life **Harold Haroldson** made his way to Norway, again likely from Ireland. He may have been with King Magnus Olafson (*aka* Magnus Barefoot or Magnus III) in 1098, maybe going on campaign to Orkney, the Isle of Man and Anglesey. Perhaps he met Skuli and Ketil in Norway (see below). Nothing more is heard. But we do hear quite a lot about Gytha, Godwin and Edmund, and three rumours about Magnus.

Magnus Haroldson possibly went to Denmark, maybe via Flanders. His future is of very vague rumours/myths of his survival, such as becoming an anchorite at Lewes, Sussex (Fig. 34), or being placed as Magnus, Count of Wrocław (Poland)[22] for which an interesting argument has been made, via the *Gesta principum Polonorum (Deeds of the Princes of the Poles)*[23] of about 1112x1118, and that this was subsequent to a marriage to a daughter of King Swein II Estridssen of Denmark. It is not dissimilar to Gytha's tale (below). What are possibly Magnus' remains were unearthed in 1966 in an archaeological dig in the ruins of a chapel in the castle at Czersk, just south of Warsaw in Poland. Czersk was within the previous Duchy of Masovia, one of a series of small states of Western Polans. Interestingly a wyvern appears in its the coat of arms. It is clearly all possible, but nothing is proven. Maybe he joined his brothers in their unsuccessful raids and was killed as per another rumour.

Figure 34. The "Magnus inscription", a Latin inscription on a semi-circular arch in the wall of St John-sub-Castro church, Lewes, East Sussex

The arch was rescued from the rubble when the old church was demolished in 1587 and erected in the wall of the new nave in 1635. It was reset, surrounding an unrelated grave slab, in the east exterior wall of the present church. The original stones, dating from around 1200, are in a medieval Lombardic script, but several have been recarved. The inscription reads:

Clauditur hic miles Danorum regia proles Mangnus nomen ei mangne nota progeniei; deponens mangnum se moribus induit agnum, prepete pro vita fit parvulus anachorita(L)
There enters this cell a warrior of Denmark's royal race; Magnus his name, mark of mighty lineage. Casting off his Mightiness he takes the Lamb's mildness, and to gain everlasting life becomes a lowly anchorite
See Pye. CC0 https://en.wikipedia.org/wiki/Magnus,_son_of_Harold_Godwinson#Tradition_of_his_survival

Gytha Haroldsdotter, thanks to the family's Danish royal connections was married off in 1074 to Vladimir II Monomakh, (figure 35) who became Great Prince of Kiev. So, Magnus' story above might just be a parallel. Kievan Rus' (figure 36) which extended from Lapland to the Black Sea was at that time a huge Viking influenced federal polity. Zajac[24] discusses Gytha's and other western marriage links to Kievan Rus' kings and princes in fascinating detail.[25] This marriage led to an ancestry to the present royal family of the United Kingdom, via King Andrew II of Hungary and descent from Harold Godwinson through his daughter, Gytha – through Kievan, Hungarian and French royal lines to Isabella of France who married Edward II, Philippa of Hainault, married to Edward III, and later Catherine of France who was grandmother of Henry VII. There is even a two-way

Figure 35. Orthodox icon of Vladimir II Monomakh. Public Domain. https://www.wikidata.org/wiki/Q60928#/media/File:Vladimir-II-Vsevolodovich_Monomakh.jpg

Scots excursion before the more recent involvement of many Germanic princes and princesses. The derived 'descent tree' from Harold to the present Royal family is below. It is all rather dependant on the early story of Gytha's marriage (in about 1069x70) accredited to the Dane, Saxo Grammaticus (about 1150 – about 1220), who may have been secretary to Absalon, Archbishop of Lund. The story is also referred to in *Fagrskinna*[26] and in Snorri Sturluson's *Heimskringla*.[27]

No primary Russian source exists, but there remained strong Scandinavian links which provide some information. Although the data is not good it is said that the oldest son Mstislav the Great was called 'Harald' in Norse sagas and his first wife[28] was Kristina Ingesdóttir, daughter of King Inge I Stenkilsson of Sweden. Their daughter, Ingeborg of Kiev, married Cnut Lavard of Jutland, and was mother to King Valdemar I of Denmark (r. 1157–82), to whom the above Absalon[29] was an influential counsellor, so this may be Saxo Gramamaticus' indirect source of the family history. The author's view is that the information must be regarded in the 'highly probable' category, but comments that the marriage of Gytha and Vladimir appears widely accepted by historians.

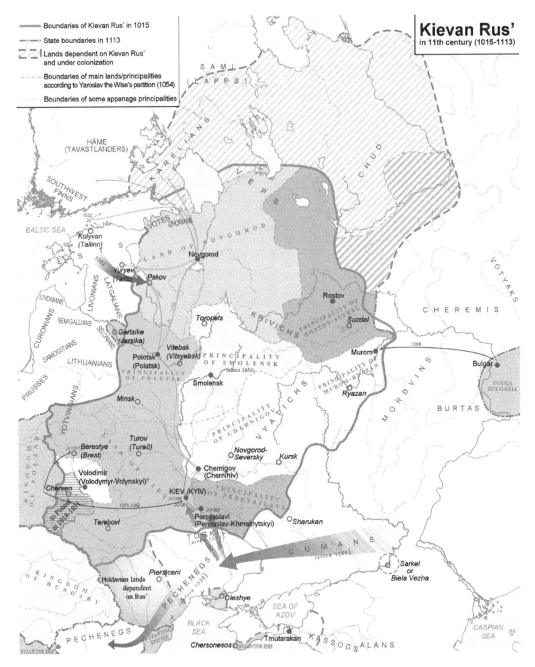

Fig. 36 Map of the Kievan Rus' realm, 1015–1113CE, of the medieval Rus' culture in Eastern Europe

CC BY S-A-2.5 from Wikimedia.

Original version (Russian): Koryakov Yuri English translation: Hellerick– http://commons.wikimedia. org/wiki/Image:Rus-1015-1113.png

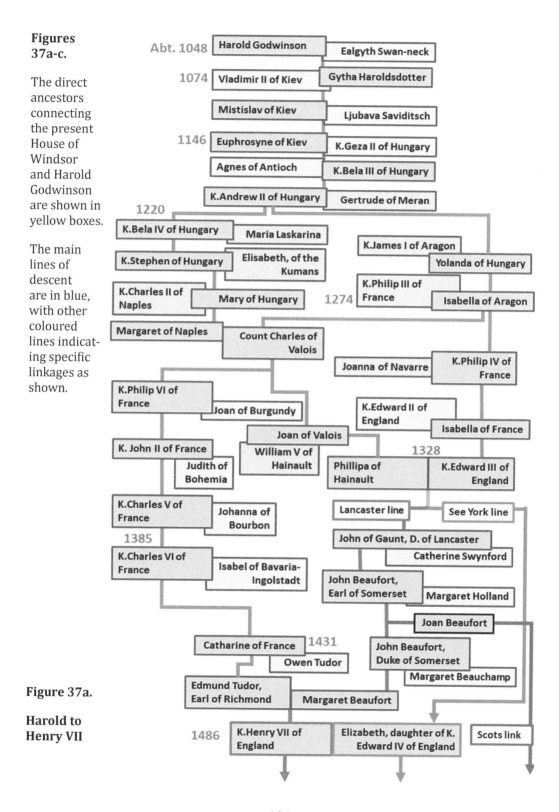

Figures 37a-c.

The direct ancestors connecting the present House of Windsor and Harold Godwinson are shown in yellow boxes.

The main lines of descent are in blue, with other coloured lines indicating specific linkages as shown.

Figure 37a.

Harold to Henry VII

Abt. 1048 — Harold Godwinson — Ealgyth Swan-neck

1074 — Vladimir II of Kiev — Gytha Haroldsdotter

Mistislav of Kiev — Ljubava Saviditsch

1146 — Euphrosyne of Kiev — K.Geza II of Hungary

Agnes of Antioch — K.Bela III of Hungary

K.Andrew II of Hungary — Gertrude of Meran

1220 — K.Bela IV of Hungary — Maria Laskarina

K.Stephen of Hungary — Elisabeth, of the Kumans

K.James I of Aragon — Yolanda of Hungary

K.Charles II of Naples — Mary of Hungary

1274 — K.Philip III of France — Isabella of Aragon

Margaret of Naples — Count Charles of Valois

Joanna of Navarre — K.Philip IV of France

K.Philip VI of France — Joan of Burgundy

K.Edward II of England — Isabella of France

Joan of Valois

K. John II of France — Judith of Bohemia — William V of Hainault

1328 — Phillipa of Hainault — K.Edward III of England

K.Charles V of France — Johanna of Bourbon

Lancaster line — See York line

John of Gaunt, D. of Lancaster — Catherine Swynford

1385 — K.Charles VI of France — Isabel of Bavaria-Ingolstadt

John Beaufort, Earl of Somerset — Margaret Holland

Joan Beaufort

Catharine of France — 1431 — Owen Tudor

John Beaufort, Duke of Somerset — Margaret Beauchamp

Edmund Tudor, Earl of Richmond — Margaret Beaufort

1486 — K.Henry VII of England — Elizabeth, daughter of K. Edward IV of England — Scots link

121

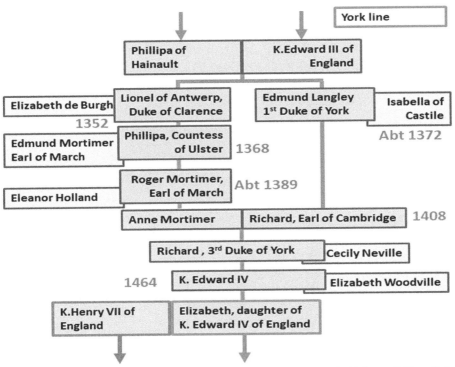

Figure 37b. The York Line, from both Phillipa of Hainault/Edward III to Princess Elizabeth of York

Notes on Figures 37 a to c
Previous page: The deduced male and female line of descent from Harold via Gytha to King Henry VII
This has interesting double lines of descent from each of King Andrew II of Hungary, Isabella of Aragon and Count Charles of Valois, the last two merging again with the marriage of King Edward III and Philippa of Hainault. There are also three consanguineous marriages – Charles of Valois with Margaret of Naples, Philippa of Hainault with Edward III of England, and also via the Lancaster line with of Edmund Tudor with Margaret Beaufort. Note the heavy involvement of French royal lines from 1274 to 1431.
This page: The York Line of descent of Elizabeth, daughter of Edward IV from Edward III
This is via two sons of Edward III, with the consanguineous marriage of Anne Mortimer and Richard of Cambridge who were 1st cousins, 3 x removed.
Next page: From Henry VII to the present Royal family, including the Scots connections
A key link here is the marriage of Joan Beaufort of the Lancastrian line with James I of Scotland, with her great grandson marrying Margaret Tudor a daughter of Henry VII and Elizabeth. Margaret carried the linking line out of England to Scotland, and it only came back to England with James I/VI. There is also a Scottish loop from James II, via his daughter Princess Mary, which gives an additional bloodline via Henry Stuart, Lord Darnley who married Mary Queen of Scots who begat James VI of Scotland/ I of England. The descent to the present time is straightforward but given the many intermarriages between the dukes, prince-electors and kings of Europe other side links almost certainly exist, but have not been further investigated here.

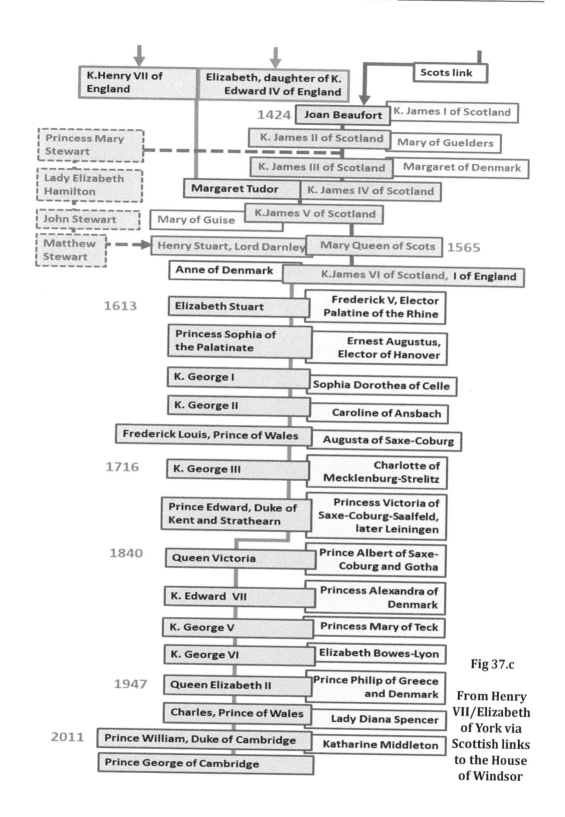

Fig 37.c

From Henry VII/Elizabeth of York via Scottish links to the House of Windsor

Godwin Haroldson and **Edmund Haroldson,** plus/minus Magnus and possibly a cousin called Tostig ended up in Ireland, in 1067. They had enough resources to ask for assistance from Dublin's King Diarmait and his son Murchad who supplied ships and mercenaries in 1068 for a raid up the Bristol Channel, to the River Avon where the Haroldsons attacked Bristol. Bristol shut its gates and the raid was unsuccessful, so they moved a short way down the Somerset coast and landed. One report suggests that 52 ships were involved, although that has been regarded as exaggerated. The local lord, Eadnoth, who had been a constable of Harold's, but had sworn allegiance to William, gathered the local forces and did battle, probably at Bleadon. There were losses on both sides and Eadnoth was killed. To make the visit worthwhile and to pay off the mercenaries the raiders plundered in Devon and Cornwall before retreating to Ireland.

The Haroldsons returned the next year in June 1069 with a fleet of 64 or 66 ships. There are varying stories about whether the raid was via the River Taw in north Devon, or River Tavy via the Tamar on the south coast and whether an attack on Exeter was also involved. It was opposed by a force based on the Devonshire fyrd, led by Brian FitzEudo, son of Eudo, Count of Brittany, who held lands in Cornwall from Robert de Mortain, and was probably based at Launceston Castle.

Interestingly the presumed progress of the plundering can be seen in the Exeter *Domesday* survey of Devon, which describes nine manors being wasted 'by Irishmen'. These were all on the south coast near Start Bay, but a good case has also been made for a north coast attack. There appear to have been two battles, and at the second the Haroldsons were significantly routed. See the separate papers by Hudson[30] and Arnold[31] for more details and references concerning the misadventures, which appear to have been big attritional raids, rather than any serious attempt to raise and lead a revolt against William. Even if that was in their minds, the way they went about things did not appear designed to win hearts.

It is probable that the death of Murchad in 1070 and of Diarmait in 1071, with the assumption of Dublin by Toirdelbach Ua Briain, who was not particularly interested in matters outside Ireland, put paid to further ventures. It is not definitely known if the Haroldsons stayed on in Ireland or made their way to Denmark to join their kin, but late sources suggest the latter. They maybe went on further east into Europe like their siblings.

In *Saga Játvarðar konungs (ON)* there is a somewhat odd story involving King William I sending 'Godwin the young, Godwin's son' as part of a mission with gifts to Swein II Estridssen, to buy off yet another Danish invasion of the North in the early 1070s. These gifts continued for a while to keep the Danes away. There is a basis of reality as William did actually pay the Danes to go away and keep away, but the above is a rambling and conflated story and surely, he was Harold's not Godwin's son, unless it was a completely different Godwin. These stories cannot be taken at face value. It would have been highly unlikely that William would have had anything to do with a Godwinson or Haroldson except to lock him up. King Swein II Estridssen died 1074x1076.

Gunnhild Haroldsdotter, born about 1055, is recorded as being at Wilton Abbey after the Conquest. She may have been there for education in 1066 and stayed there for protection. It appears that she just continued living there and had worn the abbey's habit for some time, but was never professed as a nun. William would have wished to ensure that she stayed there to avoid her marrying a rival, which might have caused future complications if she had children. Edith, the daughter of King Malcolm III and Queen Margaret of Scotland and the niece of Edgar Atheling was also incidentally at the nunnery at the same time, presumably for education. She would later marry King Henry I of England, taking the name Matilda. Dowager Queen Edith was also a regular visitor and probably died there.

Thanks to the work of Sharpe,[32] we can follow Gunnhild a bit further. He dates a probable Danish style marriage (or concubinage) of Gunnhild to Count Alan Rufus (Alan the Red), Earl of Richmond, and son of Eudo, Count of Penthièvre in Brittany, who was a second cousin of King William I, to 1072x1073.[33]

The clue that led Sharpe back to this information is a lead plaque from a tomb at Lincoln Cathedral, which is of a William d'Aincourt. A facsimile of this is below as Fig. 38. This claims that he was related to Bishop Remigius of Lincoln, formerly

Figure 38. The 'D'Eyncourt Plaque'
Copied from the publication of 1850 by d'Eyncourt, CT. *Memoir of the Leaden Plate, the Memorial of William d'Eyncourt etc.* in *'Memoirs illustrative of the History and Antiquities of the County and City of Lincoln'* at the AGM of the Archaeological Institute of Great Britain and Ireland, 1848

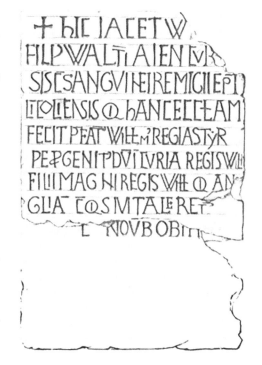

The inscription (unabbreviated) reads:
HIC IACET WILHELMUS FILIUS WALTERI AIENCURIENSIS CONSANGVINEI REMIGII EPISCOPI LINCOLIENSIS, QUI HANC ECCLESIAM FECIT. PRÆFATUS WILHELMUS, REGIA STYRPE PROGENITUS, DV(M) IN CURIA REGIS WILHELMI, FILII MAGNI REGIS WILHELMI QUI ANGLIAM CONQUISIVIT, ALERETUR, III KALENDAS NOVEMBRIS OBIIT. (L)

Here lies William, son of Walter de Aincourt related to Remigius, Bishop of Lincoln, who built this church. The aforesaid William, being of royal descent, died during the lifetime of his mother whilst being supported in the court of King William, son of the great King William who conquered England, he died on 30th October.[35]

Bishop of Dorchester (on Thames) and almoner of Fécamp Abbey, but of more import was that this William was of royal descent and had died whilst being fostered at the court of King William II Rufus. Walter D'Aincourt, father of William, had married a woman called Mathilda (b. 1073x1076) in about 1089. Sharpe has clearly shown that she was a daughter of Gunnhild and Alan Rufus, and thus a granddaughter of Harold Godwinson and Edith Swan-neck. Mathilda later and, unusually for a married woman at that time, directly gifted lands to Lincoln Cathedral and St. Marys Abbey at York; lands which had previously been those of Alan Rufus and which she could only have received from him, father to daughter.

By the birth of Mathilda, the House of Godwin was united – via the House of Brittany with the marriage of Hawise, Duke Richard I of Normandy's daughter and sister of Duke Richard II, King William I's grandfather, to Count Geoffrey I of Brittany – to the House of Normandy. The abbreviated tree showing this below as Fig. 39. Hence the information on the plaque and the access to Royal care and education.

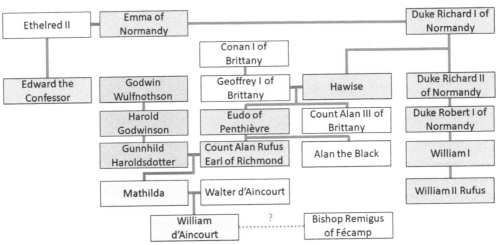

Figure 39. The English, Breton and Norman relationships of Mathilda, daughter of Gunnhilda Haroldsdotter and Alan the Red, Earl of Richmond and also of her son William d'Aincourt. ©BDHS *Red lines are marriages, blue lines the connections*

Also, what was important to Alan Rufus in marrying Gunnhild was the increased legitimisation of some of his vast landholdings,[36] which had previously belonged to Earl Edwin of Mercia, which had been added to in 1075 with Gunnhild's mother's previous holdings when the lands of Ralf de Gaël, which had been seized from Edith Swan-neck (Eddeva Pulcra) in 1069x1071, after Gaël's revolt against William in Brittany (see above) were added to Alan Rufus' huge earldom.

Alan Rufus died on 4 August 1093 and was briefly succeeded by his brother or half-brother[37] Alan Niger (Alan the Black) from whom Gunnhild sought protection. This was the time when Archbishop Anselm wrote to Gunnhild. In his first letter he implores her to return to Wilton and become a nun. Only in that way could her soul be saved, he said, by returning and professing as she had originally intended. After that they met, we do not know where or when. Clearly Gunnhild had delighted in meeting him and must have written to him to say so, and clearly had some thought of taking the veil. Anselm takes this up in his second letter of reply, saying that he had learned that she would not deny her previous holy intention. But clearly, she did not return to Wilton and died in 1097.

The d'Aincourt family itself was not inconsequential. Loyd identified that they came from Ancourt [without the i] just 7km (4 miles) from Dieppe but an older OF name for the parish is Aencourt.[38]. 'Aincurt' is found in *Domesday*. They were near neighbours of the de Warren family at Bellencombre in the Varenne[39] valley who were early supporters of William and very well rewarded in England.[40] For his support of William the Conqueror[41] Walter was also well rewarded and received 55 lordships[42] in England, mainly in Lincolnshire and Derbyshire. The precise relationship with Bishop Remigius remains unknown, but Loyd also notes that the Abbot of Fécamp was a patron of the church at A[e]ncourt, and given Regimius' history with Fécamp as a monk and almoner, the likelihood of a familial relationship is high. Twice in *Domesday* Walter d'Aincourt is referred to as 'Walter, the bishop's man', supporting this theory.

Walter d'Aincourt and Mathilda had two other sons, Walter and Ralph, and the latter became the heir, but Planché[43] tells us the male line became extinct in the '21st year of Henry VI's reign' (1442x1443).[44]

With respect to **grandchildren and great-grandchildren**, Harold Godwinson had at least one grandchild via Gunnhild, Mathilda, and via Mathilda's marriage to Walter d'Aincourt three great-grandsons, **William, Walter and Ralph d'Aincourt**, this added to the **five, possibly six grandchildren by Gytha**, one of which was **Mstislav I of Kiev**, also called **Harald** after his maternal grandfather in various Norse Sagas. Other possible grandchildren are lost in the mists of time, the green fields and mountains of Ireland, the fiords, lakes and snows of Scandinavia and the steppes of central Europe.

He had two **nephews**, sons of Tostig and Judith of Flanders, called **Skuli** and **Ketil**, who had been with their father at the Battle of Stamford Bridge, but were amongst the survivors of Hardrada's and Tostig's army and managed to take one of the few ships that returned to Norway. They settled in Norway, well looked after by King Olaf III. But they had had enough of adventures, and probably had a low opinion of Harold despite his mercy. Skuli would become an ancestor of later Norwegian kings. *Heimskringla* says,

{S} 'There came also with Olaf over the West sea, Skuli, a son of Earl Toste, and who since has been called the king's foster–son, and his brother Ketil Krok. Both were gallant men, of high family in England, and both were very intelligent; and the brothers were much beloved by King Olaf.'

But there were to be no nephews or nieces from the subject of the next section – if there had been this would have been a different story.

Last, but not least of Harold's family to consider was Harold's sister **Edith/Ealdgyth Godwinsdotter**, married to King Edward on 23 January 1045.

In this chapter we are not concerned with her life before 1066, Tostig's misadventures and Harold's death, but we should note that soon after the death of Edward and Harold's rapid coronation, therefore well before Harold's death, she took herself off to live at Winchester. This was the first part of her separation from being a Godwin to being the Dowager Queen of Edward, 'the Lady, King Edward's widow'.

But she may well have been involved, even if indirectly, with the activities of the mint at Wilton and its moneyer Centwine in continuing production of Harold II silver pennies beyond 14th October 1066. The recently discovered Chew Valley[45] hoard of coins discovered in 2019 contains 1236 Harold coins and 1310 coins of William II, the latter issued soon after his coronation. Over 100 of the Harold II coins came from the Wilton mint. Other mints involved included Bristol, Winchester and London, with a large contribution from Sussex mints.

All the post-Christmas 1066 coronation coins were of the first William I design. Because of this it is thought that the hoard was buried in the early post-Conquest period, in 1067x1068, possibly related to continuing turmoil in the south-west, possibly related to Harold's son's raids. The importance of the Wilton minted finds, as examples of symbols of authority and power, is expanded by Gareth Williams[46] who postulates that this shows the degree of independence retained by Edith in the immediate post-Conquest period leaving her poised to support any non-Norman legitimate government by Atheling Edgar or one of Harold's sons.

But in very late 1066, after the Battle of Hastings, and his loop to Dover, then round Kent to south London and Surrey, then turning through north Hampshire, through Berkshire to Oxfordshire, William had sent detachments to Winchester before he crossed the Thames at Wallingford, and subsequently moved towards London. Winchester was surrendered without any problems from the city elders or Edith, who negotiated terms and paid fealty and thus avoided looting and violence. William hence gained the English Treasury before he fully gained the country, depriving the English resisters of this huge financial resource, with which they might have recruited mercenary help. Presumably at this time unless Edith was subterfuginous and the moneyer very brave[47] the minting of Harold II coins ceased.

Aligning but not necessarily allying herself with William as the widow of Edward was an entirely pragmatic thing for Edith to do, and William I allowed her to keep her estates and income. William defined himself as the true successor to King Edward the Confessor and the concept of Edith, 'the Lady, King Edward's widow' helped with that perception. The fact that she was Harold's sister was conveniently downplayed. The one surviving post-Conquest charter known of Edith's, written in Old English describes Queen Matilda as William I's 'bedfellow'. Was there some lingering resentment to be seen in this wording, or an underhand referral back to the legitimacy of their marriage?

With her continuing retained wealth, Edith was able to maintain her patronage of English abbeys such as Wilton, as well as near continental abbeys such as Saint Riquier, and to continue to sponsor the writing of the *Vita Edwardi Regis*. This is a life of King Edward, probably scribed by a Flemish monk, most likely from Saint Bertin, a Benedictine abbey in Saint-Omer. This was started before 1066, as a general history of the Godwins and needed some prompt politically correct rewriting, redaction and revisionist editing after the Conquest. Its content suggests that its patroness did not support William fully, but also nothing after 'Hastings' suggests that she had any connection to rebellions or any part in the fates of her mother or siblings. It has been proposed that the *Vita* was completed 1067x1068.

After 1066 she lived on at Winchester and Wilton Abbey with an entirely English household until she died on 19 December 1075 at an age of about 55. Matthew Paris in his *Historia Anglorum* writing in the 13th century says: 'Yet, at the House of Winton, she struggled half alive for a long time to die'. Where did this particular, so expressive, phrase originate from? Is it possible that her drawn out illness was leprosy, and that she had at one time travelled to or been in communication with the Abbey of La Chaise-Dieu in search of a cure, as advanced above in the section about Ealdgyth of Mercia?

William ensured she was buried next to Edward in Westminster Abbey, which maintained the 'Edward's consort illusion' that had been created. When a new shrine was constructed in 1269 she was reburied on its left-hand side, but nothing marks her tomb. If it was ever reopened, might we find that her bones bear at least one the osseous stigmata of leprosy, i.e., periostitis, chronic osteitis, osteomyelitis and dactylitis?

She is one of only three women depicted on the *Bayeux Tapestry*, in her case in Edward's death bed scene. Carola Hicks[48] argued that she, not Odo of Kent, was the *BT's* patron, a view not heavily supported, but which to the author of this book would re-raise the question of some possible role of Wilton Abbey vis à vis the production of the *BT.*

The Prior of Winchester Cathedral, Godfrey of Cambrai (bef.1055–1107), would later write as an epitaph:

> The nobility of your forbears magnified you, O Edith,
> And you, a king's bride, magnify your forbears.
> Much beauty and much wisdom were yours
> And also probity together with sobriety.
> You teach the stars, measuring, arithmetic, the art of the lyre,
> The ways of learning and grammar.

An understanding of rhetoric allowed you to pour out speeches,
And moral rectitude informs your tongue.
The sun burned for two days in Capricorn
When you discarded the weight of your flesh and went away.

With these last words about Edith the few and somewhat uncertain facts that we have about Harold's family after 'Hastings' run out. There is no hint in these family histories that Harold had not died at Hastings and the Godwin family was in no position to try to make any sort of comeback. But the House of Normandy only felt totally secure in England until after 1100, once Henry I was on the throne.

Notes

1   The original church at Bruges was destroyed by fire in 1116 but rebuilt. The story of the jewels may be a myth.

2   Saint Saviour's became the cathedral after the destruction of Saint Donatien. The final remains of Saint Donatien's church lie under a hotel in Bruges city centre and can be visited via the hotel's basement.

3   Knowles, Dom D., Brooke, CNL. and London, V. *The Heads of Religious Houses: England and Wales 940–1216* (1972)

4   This makes interpretation difficult at times. Norman scribes were not noted for their consistency when recording English (or Norman for that matter) names.

5   Hailesaltede Hundred would later split North/South as Netherfield/Battle half-Hundreds.

6   *PASE Domesday*'s 'Eadgifu 24. Here there are 217 entries. 64 of which are related to Cambridgeshire, with another 18 in Suffolk, 11 in Essex , nine in Lincolnshire and a combined 27 in Buckinghamshire and Hertfordshire confirming an East Anglian focus. Other notable entries were in Sussex (11) and Yorkshire (12)

7   'OE *pulchra*' = '*beautiful*'. Identified by Boyle in 1896 and quoted by Sharpe in 2007 and Keats-Rohan in 2012.

8   One rumour has it that she lived a quiet, holy life and was buried at Stortford in Hertfordshire.

9.   *PASE*'s 'Ealdgyth 2'. She has only a few relationship entries. She is recorded as 'Aldgyth' in *Domesday* as having held Binley, Warwickshire. It was worth £3. In 1086 it was the property of St. Mary's Abbey, Coventry having been bought by the local Bishop from Ealdgyth's son in law, Osborn fitzRichard. Nothing else is found.

10   Edwin and Morcar both survived the Conquest but would later rebel. Edwin was killed in 1071. Morcar was eventually imprisoned in Normandy, released on William's death and re-imprisoned by William Rufus at Winchester, where he is presumed to have died as no more is heard of him.

11   French guidebooks to the Auvergne say that one of three monumental tombs in the north aisle of the abbey church of St Robert's choir contains the body of an English 'Queen Edith'. However, they also say that it is thought to be Edith, widow of King Edward the

Confessor, which seems impossible as her body lies in Westminster Abbey.

12   Baxter, S. *The Earls of Mercia – Lordship and Power in late Anglo-Saxon England* (2007).

13   Beech, G. 'England and Aquitaine in the century before the Norman Conquest' *Anglo-Saxon England* 19 (1990).

14   Gaussin, P-R. *L'Abbaye de la Chaise-Dieu (1043–1518) – L'abbaye en Auvergne et son rayonnement dans la Chrétienté* (1962).

15   The whole story is rather complex, Edward the Confessor's Queen Edith may have had some involvement with La Chaise-Dieu.

16   Le jour de feste des Trépassés, il se trouve, dans l'ancien coustumier de ceste abbaye, que l'on doibt faire commémoraison pour l'ame d'une royne d'Angleterre, pour avoir faict bastir* le dourtoir de ladicte abbaye; il est croiable que c'est pour celle qui fust guérie de la lèpre par les mérites et prières de nostre sainct Adelelme qui, sans doùbte, voulut faire ce bienfaict au monastère duquel ledit sainct estoit sorty. (OF)

On All Souls' Day, it is found, in the old customary of this abbey, that a commemoration should be made for the soul of a queen of England, for having allowed to be built the dorter (dormitory) of the said abbey; It is believed that it is for the one who was cured of leprosy by the merits and prayers of our Saint Adelelm who, without doubt, wanted to do this good for the monastery, which the said saint has left.* (Author's translation)

*Edward's Queen Edith gave money for this it is said, see text.

17   Gardon, F. *Histoire de l'abbeye de la Chaise-Dieu* (17th century, published 1912). Available on-line at BnF.

18   Adelelm (*Adelème in modern French*) was of noble birth from Loudun. He became a soldier. After the death of his parents, he sold his inheritance and undertook a pilgrimage to Rome. The renown of the founder, Abbot Robert de Turlande of the Abbey de La Chaise-Dieu, persuaded him to become a monk. He became master of the novices and in 1078 abbot, but he left later that year for Spain at the request of King Alphonse VI to assist in the reconquest of Spain from the Muslims at the time of El Cid, to re-introduce the rites of Rome. Alphonse built him a priory at Burgos (of San Juan), a daughter house of La Chaise-Dieu, now in ruins. He died in Spain, where he had continued to perform miracles.

19   Queen Matilda, William I's wife, after a severe rift with William following her ill-advised support of her son Robert in 1077–78, sent to Saint Adelelm who was by then in Spain, to send her some blessed bread that reportedly cured her 'lethargy'.

20   Son of Richard fitzScrobe, called Richard Scrope in *Open Domesday*, Richard Scrob in *PASE*, a Norman who had come to England in Edward the Confessor's time, possibly with Ralf the Timid, and had been granted lands in Herefordshire, building Richards Castle, near Ludlow, one of very few pre-Norman castles. Also see *PASE* Osbern10 fitzRichard and Osbern16 fitzScrob. Osbern 10 inherited by marriage to Nest/Nesta the manor of Bistre, Cheshire which had once belonged to Gruffydd ap Llewellyn, (PASE's Gruffudd 1) and had passed to his mother-in-law

21   Near Llanfechan in mid-Wales, itself near Builth Wells. See Jones, T. *The Chronicle of the Princes* (1955)

22   Magnus of Wroclaw is discussed in some detail in Skarbek-Kozietulski, M. 'More about Magnus, Count of Wroclaw', *Genealogia Mediaevalis Genetica*, (2011) via https://www.academia.edu

23   Authored by Gallus Anonymous.

24   Zajac, NAM. *Women Between West and East: The Inter-Rite Marriages of the Kyivan Rus' Dynasty, ca. 1000–1204*. PhD Thesis, Centre for Medieval Studies, University of Toronto (2017)

25   The conflict between the western brides' Catholicism and their husbands' Orthodoxy is a particular topic.

26   *Fagrskinna* is one of the Norwegian kings' sagas, written around 1220.

27   *Heimskringla*, also written down in about 1220, is collection of sagas of the early Norwegian kings, written in Old Norse.

28   Gytha's (and therefore Harold's) line of descent to the present UK Royal family is through Mstislav's second wife, Ljubava, the daughter of Dmitry Saviditsch, of Novgorod.

29   The city of Copenhagen venerates him as its founder, it is said that he was one of the best Scandinavian prelates of the time. He was also a warrior archbishop.

30   Hudson, B. 'The Family of Harold Godwinson and the Irish Sea Province,' *Journal of the Royal Society .of Antiquaries of Ireland.* Vol. 109, 92–100 (1979)

31   Arnold, N. 'The Defeat of the sons of Harold in 1069' *Battalia,* Vol.1 (2017) ISSN 2516-0451.

32   Sharpe, R. 'King Harold's Daughter' in North, W. and Morillo, S. (Ed.) *Haskins Society Journal XIX – Studies in Medieval History* (2008 for 2007)

33   The reason for suggesting that it was not a conventional marriage is that at Alan Rufus' death neither Gunnhild nor her daughter inherited his lands, which passed to his brother.

34   DVP or DVM is used for death within a father's or mother's lifetime. Here the overline ¯ to the V extends the text to DVM. The female version is probably used because of Mathilda's status.

35   Converted from the Roman calendar. We are not given the year, it may have been just after the death of Remigius in 1092, but before Rufus' death in 1100.

36   In 1086 he was the fourth largest lay tenant in chief in England.

37   His father Eudo of Penthièvre sired at least 20 children, not all by his wife.

38   See Longnon. *Pouillés de la province de Rouen* (a register of churches etc.).

39   The River Varenne is a tributary of the River Arques which reaches the sea at Dieppe.

40   Thanks to Claire de Warren, a member of BDHS, for sight of her family history *Histoire de la Maison de Warren* by Geoffroy de Warren. The de Warren family also had some possessions at Ancourt.

41   Maybe as Ancourt is so near Arques la Bataille he (and possibly the de Warrens) could have assisted in Duke William's Siege of Arques in 1053 as well as at the Conquest?

42   Maybe as many as 70 according to Open Domesday.

43   Planché, JR, *The Conqueror and his Companions*, Vol 2 (1874).

44   Sir John Deincourt, 5th Lord Deincourt, only had daughters, Margaret and Alice.

45   In North Somerset, almost equidistant from Bristol, Bath and Weston super Mare. Quite near Bleadon.

46   Williams, G. 'Was the last Anglo-Saxon King of England a Queen? A possible posthumous Coinage of Harold II' The Yorkshire Numismatist IV (2012).

47   Penalties for forging etc. were draconian.

48   Hicks, C. *The Bayeux Tapestry: The Life Story of a Masterpiece* (2007)

Part II

It's all Harold's Fault

We have no need to read fairy stories, for the true stories of history are infinitely more devious, enthralling and full of interest than fiction.

Interpretations of the Norman Conquest from before 1066 until today

Introduction to Part 2

Interpretations in Britain of the long-term effects of Harold's defeat and the subsequent Norman Conquest, ever since the immediate post-Conquest period until the beginning of the 21st century, have varied significantly. These interpretations were and remain influenced by concurrent dynastic and geopolitical, economic social criteria and visions as well as conspiracy theorists, alternative history promoters, and historical fiction of varying quality. The early periods after '1066' until the end of the Feudal period in the early 14th century also need to take into account the imported Norman paradigms which had evolved before and during William's dukedom.

Seldom has any great rigour or critical questioning been attached to these varied constructs until towards the end of the 19th century; indeed, sometimes it could even be personally dangerous for historians to try to use such tools. History could not be regarded as a nearly dispassionate science until after the dawn of the 20th century; it still cannot be regarded as totally dispassionate today as there are always interpretive disagreements over matters on which there can never be agreement, as the evidence is inadequate.

There has been a plethora of myths, chronicles, charters, manuscripts, discussions, books, views, academic papers, radio and television programmes, films, and internet forums with quite a lot of misinterpretation and misinformation about the Norman Conquest, overlayed by a copious corpus of historical fiction which has a precarious use of facts.

Sometimes the misinterpretation or misinformation is opportunistic and/or deliberate, sometimes innocent because of error, when applied to the events before, during and after the Conquest since the day after the Battle of Hastings. Possibly that is about all we can be certain about in this long-standing debate. The underlying issue is that many of the 'original' numerous written sources, communications and interpretations have unfortunately been biased or controversial or have errors and conflictions, and later conflations sometimes with two or three of the four or all four:

enough to confuse all who have searched for the many elusive facts.

The Anglo-Saxon world, already influenced since the 8th century by Danes who had settled in the north and east of England, had become even more influenced by people from Scandinavian backgrounds from the 10th century, when Ethelred II 'the Unraed' – which itself means ill-advised or ill-counselled, rather than 'unready' – a deliberate Victorian construct – married Emma of Normandy in 1002. She had arrived in England with an attendant train of Normans, descended in part from Danish Vikings. This influence became even greater after the accession by conquest to the English throne of the Danish King Cnut in 1016 and his political marriage to the same Emma.

Then, after the short interlude of relative chaos following the death of Cnut in 1035 (when his Anglo-Scandinavian son Harold I Harefoot (d.1040) and Norman-Scandinavian son Harthacnut (d.1042) were kings of England), the Anglo-Norman Edward the Confessor, the son of Ethelred II and Emma, was crowned.

About 30 years of Edward's childhood and early adult life had been spent in Normandy in exile, and this long period must have coloured his mindset for his lifetime. When he came to England, he brought a significant number of his Norman friends and advisors with him, and placed them in positions of influence, causing tensions particularly with Earl Godwin of Wessex.

The great English earldoms also had distinctive characteristics which meant that England was not quite the uniform kingdom it may have seemed from the outside and from the cushion of nearly 1,000 years of time. But a common law had been established – for example via Edgar's code, issued in 962–63. This specifically talks about:

> ... measures common to all the nation, whether English, Danes, or Britons, in every province of my kingdom, to the end that poor man and rich may possess what they rightly acquire ...

And the laws of Edgar were chosen in the reign of Cnut by both people of Danish and English origin at a 'Great Meeting' at Oxford in 1018.

The English king and nobility made the laws, but village communities and family ties were strong and helped enforce the law at a local level, so crime and punishment were normally dealt with within local hundreds. Anglo-Saxon justice relied heavily on religion when deciding whether someone was guilty or innocent, and oaths played an important part in proving innocence. Hearings took place in public. If there was uncertainty trial by ordeal could take place. Punishments could include execution, mutilation, slavery and fines.

The Norman duchy had seen a parallel development following immigration of Danes into western Neustria (the western part of the kingdom of the Franks, now France), from about 800 when the area around the River Seine and Rouen was colonised. There were not huge numbers of immigrants in relative terms, but they married local Frankish women, and this was followed by a surprisingly rapid spread across Normandy with assimilation and some submergence of their Old Norse language with the western Franks. The institutions and customs of the duchy remained essentially Frankish, with some input from Scandinavian justice systems.

Neustria covered the northern part of France within the Frankish empire in the 9th century. As early as the beginning of the 10th century oral legal customs evolved – *La Coutume de Normandie* – which were progressively refined in the 11th and 12th centuries and remained in use with further developments including influences from the Anglo-Norman realm of England in the 12th century, and with other French modifications until the French Revolution when there was extensive recodification. Besmier[1] and Neveux[2] both describe this evolution. Elements of *La Coutume* persist in the Channel Islands, the last bit of Normandy under British control, with some effects on law and language there.

The Battle of Hastings of 14th October 1066 was the result of political and dynastic events which had occurred mainly over the previous century, which are précised in *1066 and the Battle of Hastings – Preludes, Events and Postscripts*. It could even be considered that the Battle of Hastings was fought between Anglo-Danes aka the English and Franco-Danes aka the Normans (with the blessing of Pope Alexander II[3] and plenty of mercenary help to the Normans from Franks, the Flemish and Bretons).

No list of the '100 most decisive battles of the world' would exclude the Battle of Hastings. The English-speaking world cannot forget the date as the authors of *1066 and all that* exploited.[4] The battle was fought for the crown of England on an empty hillside with a sandy ridge at a natural bottleneck – on the only landside way out of what was then a Hastings peninsula – by ancient track crossroads at an anonymous place to be called simply 'La Bataille', after the event – which has become 'Battle'.

'Hastings' marked the English beginning of the Norman Conquest, which event would influence the English-speaking world over centuries, with echoes even today. Not only that, but it would also indirectly affect, for good or bad, many other peoples who had the fortune or misfortune to encounter that English-speaking world.

Progress after the Conquest to homogenisation of the two cultures would be slow. The old English and new Norman French languages would not suddenly meld to become 'middle English'. This would take a considerable time, as conquerors and conquered did not have a great deal of social intercourse. The post-Hastings progress of Norman settlement and acculturation of England would initially be brutal, but later move to a more positive developmental phase. It would never develop as rapidly as Normandy itself had developed by acculturation because in England it was a definitive takeover of crown, government and land. The Normans, whilst numerically well outnumbered, remained the elite and prime force in the land for a long time.

Holding at first by force and awesome castle building, they also moved on to use more or less subtle spiritual means as abbey, church and cathedral building gathered momentum to match that which they had achieved in Normandy at places like Jumièges, Rouen, Bec, Caen and Fécamp. Cathedrals like Durham and Ely, built after rebellions, were powerful weapons of occupation with the clear statement 'We are here to stay.' English archbishops and bishops were fairly quickly replaced by Norman clergy and Normans were the abbots of the new monasteries. They became extensive landholders at the expense of local English earls, thanes and yeomen in much the same way as the secular warlike followers of William I had prospered.

It was now the Normans who wrote and enforced the laws in England, but there was continuity of local English laws via the hundreds and a few higher-ranking English were on non-baronial local juries. Trial by combat was added to the list of ordeals by fire or water if innocence or guilt could not be easily determined, but later this was supplanted by inquest juries with jurors drawn from the local area, a development from Frankish law. Forest law with draconian punishments for trespass and poaching was introduced, which was particularly resented by the English. Norman French was the ruling language of power, but Old English was never suppressed.

It is worth briefly stepping back before 1066 to review the way, firstly in which the Norman system of military service and administration had developed and, secondly, how it changed after William had full control of his duchy, once rebellions had settled down. It was William's evolved version that was implemented in England after the Conquest, once he realised that the English were not going to just roll over and accept him with open arms. This was at a level above the mainly continuing English laws, although there was never any 'perfect pyramid' of organisation.

So just how did the Norman Conquest come to be viewed by the population and historians on the northern side of the English Channel down the centuries? The periods when distinctly different perspectives can be seen are divided as follows:

Norman preludes – before and after William became Duke, then
- Conquest through to the early mediaeval period.
- The later Medieval period until the Dissolution of the Monasteries
- Post-Dissolution: 1538 to the end of the Tudors.
- The reigns of the Stuarts and the interregnum.
- From the Glorious Revolution to the end of the Industrial Revolution.
- The Victorian era.
- Early 20th century.
- The late 20th century
- The 21st century

Prelude to 1066: Before Duke William II (before 1035)

Firstly, to understand how things evolved we should look at the time before Duke William II's Norman way (with thanks to François Neveux whose description of the 'feudal' arrangements both before and after William's changes has been translated from the French and contextualised by the author).

Normandy before the time of Duke William II had developed an hierarchical society. The next in order of precedence to the duke in the aristocracy were his tenants-in-chief or barons or seigneuries. Often heading several baronies, they each had dependent large numbers of knights, but quite deliberately their lands were scattered across the duchy, to reduce the potential for coalescence of large seigneuries in a single block, which might seriously threaten the authority of the duke. The only notable exception to this was the barony of Bellême, east of Alençon and north-east of Le Mans, on the border between Normandy and Anjou where the baron's fiefs (estates of land held with feudal obligations of military service) were defensively clustered. The barons paid direct homage to the duke, and many had family ties to the ducal family, and with each other via intermarriages.

Under the barons each knight would hold a fief at a secondary level. This fief had to provide the resources for the equipment and maintenance of mounted warriors, able to give at least 40 days of service per year, which was very expensive. In addition, he had to live a 'noble' life. This meant that the knight's fief would normally have to cover an area of between 200 and 600 hectares (2 to 6 square kilometres or 500 to 1500 acres or ¾ to 2¼ square miles) to provide the sort of income required. Presumably, the area required would also have been somewhat dependent on the nature of the terrain, its agricultural value, etc.

Under the knight's fief existed the vavassorie, which usually corresponded to a fraction of a fief. A vavasseur was essentially an under-vassal with military obligations similar to those of the knight, sometimes with a riding horse but more normally providing a horse for transport purposes. The local administration was originally entrusted to the barons and their viscounts (sheriffs) who carried out administrative duties, policing, and justice.

Prelude to 1066: William's Norman Way; 1035–1066

William, son of Duke Robert I, acceded to the duchy in 1035 at the age of only seven. By 1037 his regency council had weakened, and barons were engaging in bloody private wars. Fortunately, sometime after 1040 King Henri I of France intervened to help William in his capacity as overlord. There followed a series of peace councils, from about 1042, and things held together until Guy of Burgundy, a cousin, son of his aunt Alice, sister of Duke Robert, led a coup. This was thwarted at the Battle of Valès-Dunes in 1047 which was followed by a more rigorous but uneasy 'Truce of God'. By 1054 William, aged about 27, had good control of Normandy but Henri started to believe that he was becoming a threat to the kingdom of France. William then withstood French assaults and put down a few more baronial revolts. By 1060 he was in full control. A fuller description of events can be found in *1066 and the Battle of Hastings*.

Duke William II made his significant changes to the governance of Normandy as soon as he was able (presumably starting in about 1054) to reduce the independence of the warring barons. Incidentally, this may have been the cause of some localised baronial revolts against loss of some independence, but all of these were eventually put down, firmly.

By 1060, only the Counts of Eu, Evreux and Mortain remained fully trusted ducal family members. The rest of the duchy was divided into counties with viscounts (sheriffs) directly administering ducal affairs and finances and responsible solely to William, although the barons retained their own sheriffs for specific local affairs. In the south-west this system was pragmatically and strategically somewhat less developed with more retention of local powers.

The viscounts now exercised ducal administrative powers, policing, and justice in their areas. They commanded the troops conscripted for the ducal army and as castle guards. On the financial side, they were assisted by lower ranking personnel – the 'graverie' who collected direct ducal tax; the 'tonlieu', responsible for collecting indirect taxes; and 'forestarii', foresters responsible for the ducal forests.

The operation of the military system was possible only because it was backed by a well-organised ducal administrative organization, which used a rudimentary but efficient calculator, using tokens and boxes, looking somewhat like a chessboard, later called an 'Exchequer'.

Conquest to early Mediaeval: 1066 to 1204

This was the system that William introduced to England after the Conquest, with barons' landholdings scattered across the country, except in strategic defensive areas. Around the south coast and the Welsh and Scottish borders he used the Norman model of the frontier comptés like Mortain, Eu and Évreux to set up strong baronies under one well trusted baron: the Count of Eu in the Rape of Hastings, for instance, (see Foord, *The Rapes of Sussex, Hundreds of Hastings Rape and the people of the Rape of Hastings to 1538*).

He also used county sheriffs to keep an eye on royal finances, justice, and administration. Even so, imbalances of power could still develop as barons could exhibit 'an extravagant and self-interested hooliganism' for self-enhancement (Fleming).

In France, the underlings were subject to *'la Coutume de Normandie'* and in

England *'basic custumal English law'* which was maintained for English local land and justice administration although later there was some merging of the two codes started by Henry II.

Under Henry I, Normandy and England were reunited after the spats between William II Rufus and Robert Curthose, and then between Henry I and Robert Curthose. After that up until 1204, there was no clear top level separate administration for the kingdom and for the duchy. The main innovation was the introduction of a 'justicier of Normandy' who was the representative of the king in the duchy whilst the king was in England. This post was first held by Jean, Bishop of Lisieux (1107–1141) who had been a royal chaplain and belonged to Henry's family group. For Norman justice there was of a group of itinerant officers who were called 'justiciers'.

During the reign of Henry I (r.1100–1135) what was definitively put into place were the financial organizations and judicial systems that would develop and fully manifest themselves in England under the name of 'Exchequer' at the time of the Plantagenets, after the reign of Stephen.

It was mostly Norman monks who wrote the laudatory (panegyric) early histories of the victors. English perspective histories of 1066 and the subsequent violent years of 'shock and awe' are sparse and only developed sometime later as acculturation progressed. By Domesday in 1086 it is estimated that (in approximate terms) 20% of the land was held by William or the royal family, Norman barons held 48%, the church (which had had a Norman takeover) 26% and only about 6% by pre-Conquest landowners, not all of whom were English, as this would have included holders like the Abbaye de Fécamp. This pattern can be seen in the listings for eastern Sussex in *BC to 1066*. English monks and clerics were highly unlikely to obtain promotions. By 1086 there were only four significant English tenants-in-chief and in 1087 Wulfstan of Worcester was the only remaining English bishop. In addition, Norman merchants were widespread in England and usually received more favourable arrangements than their English counterparts with respect to local tenancies and taxes.

The Norman Conquest had been a culturally and physically violent and extensive takeover indeed, probably to all intents and purposes cemented by 1072, when it has been estimated that the English finally realised that they had no way back. The *ASC* entries for the immediate post-Conquest years are notably terse and brief.

There were small signs of early assimilation as by 1090 William's son, William II Rufus, sent for Englishmen under the command of sheriffs to fight his brother Robert Curthose for the control of his father's new empire, rather than rely on Norman lords' split loyalties. But note the phrase 'under the command of sheriffs'. These sheriffs were still Normans, local administrators and law enforcers, their equivalents were known in Normandy as 'vicomtes', although there were some significant dissimilarities between the functions of English sheriffs and Norman vicomtes.[5] In the Rape of Hastings, a man called Reinbert was an early sheriff responsible to the lord of the Rape, Robert, Count of Eu. He did well and in turn held much land from Eu, becoming the progenitor of the Etchingham family.

Early Norman lords did marry Englishwomen, but mainly to cement their hold on lands. For example Robert D'Oyly married Ealdgyth, the daughter of Wigod of Wallingford. After Wigod's death, Robert D'Oyly held property in Wallingford 'iure uxos' (L) (*by the right of his wife*). The differentiation between Norman aristocrats and their retinues and their subject local English populations would break down only very slowly. At the end of the 12th century David Bates notes that, even at that time about 125 years after the Conquest, the upper levels of the aristocracy remained almost impenetrable to those of English birth and descent and that Norman networks remained strong across England and Normandy, including cross-Channel networks. The Norman imperial elite remained in position until the feudal system broke down, but well before that social mobility gradually became the norm both locally and regionally at lower social levels.

Later Medieval period until the Dissolution: 1204–1538

French initially remained the language of the rulers, but this French became an 'Anglo-Norman' dialect, eventually mocked by Frenchmen who found the words and accents of those who attempted to speak 'French' hilarious or bizarre. With intermarriage and the passing of the years, Norman-French and the Old English languages coexisted, but then slowly intermingled and Middle English evolved to became dominant in secular life.

At first the clerical scribes had written their histories in Latin, but two generations later Anglo-French started to be used, followed by more works in Middle English from the 13th century. By the late 1300s teaching of children of every status was in Middle English. Latin and Norman-French histories started to be translated to English.

The Plantagenet Empire which followed 'the Anarchy' of Stephen's rule in England, broke down towards the end of the 13th century, accelerated by King John's many errors. But much of the Norman network remained intact and many barons had cross-Channel interests, although they had started to lose control of their destinies. Many had to decide if they were to continue in England or in Normandy alone. Countess Alix d'Eu was to lose Hastings when she opted for her estates in Normandy in preference to those, including the Rape of Hastings, in England.

Taxation in England was high and post-1204 change was in the air as the English-Norman barons moved in on a weak King John and demanded more control of affairs. This led to the Magna Carta of 1215 which stated the right of the barons to consult and advise the king in his Great Council. This John rapidly persuaded Pope Innocent III to revoke. When King John suddenly died in 1216, his heir Henry III (b.1207–r.1216–d.1272) was only nine years old, and the Earl of Pembroke, William Marshal, acted as regent until Henry III came of age. Marshal issued a modified Magna Carta on 12th November 1216 and a further revision on 6th November 1917. In 1225 King Henry

III made yet more revisions and reissued the charter, and 1236 saw the earliest use of the term 'Parliament', referring to the Great Council. The 1225 version of *Magna Carta* officially became part of English law in 1297.

The system of interconnecting feudal obligations was still there but starting to break down significantly in England, even before the Peasants Revolt of 1381. Payments of money began to replace the original obligation of armed service. Fiefs became mainly hereditary, reducing the link between vassal and lord.

To use once more the example of the Rape of Hastings, the Eu family held it from 1070 until Countess Alix d'Eu elected to retain her possessions in France in 1243x44 over those in England. After that, the Rape passed in 1268 to the Duke of Brittany (a duchy still separate from Normandy and an inconstant ally of England), who was also Earl of Richmond, and through the hands of subsequent dukes/earls until forfeited in 1341.

Henry IV (r.1399–1413) was perhaps the first king of England for whom English was the language of choice. He was behind the curve for, before him, from 1362 all pleas in the law courts and, from 1363, the majority of discussions in parliament had to be conducted in English.

Because early medieval histories were so full of myths, poetic licence,

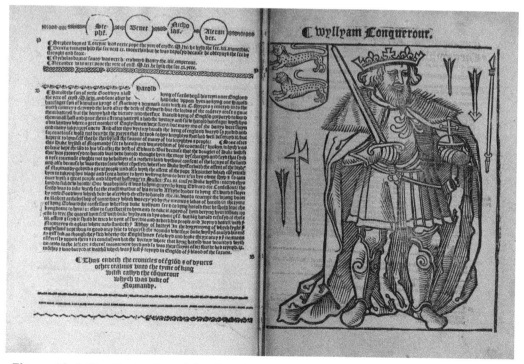

Figure 40. A Woodcut print of the '1066' pages in Rastell's book 'Pastyme of Peoples'
From: https://archive.org/details/pastymeofpeoplec00rast/page/n1/mode/2up

exaggerations of events and prowess, misplaced praise, and references back to the sometimes dubious one-sided post-1066 Norman histories, which often had multiple revisions and embroideries, they were and unfortunately remain, an abundant source of varying interpretations and misinterpretation particularly if read selectively and uncritically. It says it all that in Henry VIII's reign his 'scholarly' advisors, led by Bishop Edward Foxe, used these faulty ancient texts to mine for arguments during his initial unsuccessful attempts to divorce Catherine of Aragon.

John Rastell included the Norman Conquest in his book *'Pastyme of Peoples'* in 1529, (Fig.40) which contained curious Tudor English nationalistic theories about the feudal age. Rastell married Elizabeth More, sister of the Catholic martyr Sir Thomas More, but became a Protestant who was never completely trusted and died in 1536. He was an MP and has an 'interesting' entry in the *History of Parliament web pages*.

Post-Dissolution to the end of the Tudor era: 1538–1603

After the dissolution lay people became more widely educated, printing became established, and many manuscripts became available from dissolved monasteries and later found their way into various collectors' libraries, such as the Cottonian Collection made by Sir Robert Bruce Cotton MP (1571–1631) (Fig.41). French and Latin histories were translated into English and de nova English histories were produced, usually curious mixtures of invention, extracts from translated old chronicles and even legend. Marjorie Chibnall says William of Malmesbury's and Henry of Huntingdon's 12th century writings were 'roughly cobbled together' for these printings. Shakespeare wrote his *'Histories'*, which were mainly fiction, based on a little history. Fortunately, they did not include a *'William I'*.

Figure 41. A reproduction bust of Sir Robert Bruce Cotton
Blwa51 British Library (Public Domain)

A peculiar form of regal and legal old French (OF) persisted, remarkably still seen today in the words 'la reyne/le roy le veult' (*trans. the queen/king wishes it*) signifying in the UK Parliament that a public bill (including a private member's bill) has received royal assent from the monarch of the United Kingdom. It was only in 1971 that travelling 'assize' (OF: assise [*trans. sessions or sitting*]) courts, one of whose commissions was 'ayer and terminer' (OF trans: *to hear and to determine*), were abolished by the Courts Act of 1971 and replaced by permanent crown courts. The town crier's *'Oyez, Oyez'* (*'Hear me, Hear me'*) is another small survival.

Judgements on the value of the history of the Norman Conquest veered strongly in royalist directions during Tudor times and avoided discussing earlier rebellious phases. In these tense and suspicious times these could have drawn dangerous attention to the authors' underlying possibly treasonous motives. But the absence of male heirs caused some active interest to be taken by Henry VIII's researchers into his forebear Henry I's manoeuvrings when he was trying to make his daughter Mathilda his heir – or at least create a precedent for the crown to be passed onward via the female line if there was no direct male heir.

Histories of ecclesiastical authority and freedom of conscience were Tudor tiger territory, to be avoided, if one wished to keep one's head or avoid being burnt to death as a heretic.

The reigns of the Stuarts and the Interregnum: 1603–1688

Once the Stuarts took over and during the Commonwealth interregnum the debate moved to weighty thoughts on constitutional issues and on understanding the effects that the Norman Conquest had had on both an imagined pre-Conquest ancient 'constitution' of the kingdom, and some sort of illusory post-Conquest parliament. Cue the involvement of lawyers, parliamentarians, and scholars, mostly serious but some not so or ideological or swayed by popular opinions.

This foment found no evidence that the English Witangemot had had any ancient 'constitution' although it had provided an ad hoc gathering of available senior earls and clerics to proffer advice if asked and to consensually support the king's wishes, and no writs summoning representation of the 'commons' could be found from before Henry III's reign. This is, of course, highlights another source of variance in any historical story – no record, no verité.

The preposterous myth that the pre-Conquest English had all existed as some sort of free and equal citizens in some kind of rural utopia was rightly extinguished. So an ancient parliament that for some reason had become imagined from older untrustworthy writings such as the *'Laws of King William'* and the *'Laws of Edward the Confessor'* (both called by Robert Brady 'an incoherent farce and mixture and a heap of nonsense'... see below) had not been subverted by the Norman Conquest.

What had happened was that the Norman 'feudal' system with Norman laws and customs at organizational and administrative levels had basically been imposed on top of local traditional English law. From that evolved 'feudal obligations' over land tenure, wardship, marriage, military services. etc., all of which if disputed, initially by Normans against their overlords, involved the legal system which evolved the concepts of precedents and outcomes of prior litigation so beloved of lawyers to this day.

John Hayward produced perhaps the first textbook about the Conquest in 1613.

Then in 1623 John Selden edited and published Eadmer's *'Historia Novorum'* and in 1629 Henry Spelman initiated a study of feudalism when he wrote *'Feuds and Tenures by Knight Service'*.

It is interesting to note that the Cottonian Library was closed in 1629–1633[6] on the orders of Charles I – in case it contained items from the past which could be used against the monarchy.

Such was the turmoil during the interregnum and afterwards that thoughts of earlier histories beyond religious history became obscured, but the The Royal Society of London for Improving Natural Knowledge, to become the Royal Society was founded on 28 November 1660, and was granted a royal charter by King Charles II

The Glorious and Industrial Revolutions: 1688–1837

With the debut of the multidisciplinary Royal Society and particularly after the Glorious Revolution of 1688, international contacts improved and debates about the past moved to a less political and more serious intellectual level.

Robert Brady produced *'A Complete History of England'* critically using old chronicles, some cartularies, *Domesday*, and the Close, Patent and Charter Rolls. Sir Mathew Hale, a respected Chief Justice between 1671 and 1676 contributed a *History of the Common Law* which was published posthumously. Anglo-Saxon studies advanced and Thomas Rymer made accessible previously secret treaties in the *Foedera*, a collection of 'all the leagues, treaties, alliances, capitulations, and confederacies, which have at any time been made between the Crown of England and any other kingdoms, princes and states, and other documents concerning foreign relations. Thomas Madox followed up by making available in the *Formulare Anglicanum* many hundreds of charters, following the French cleric Mabillon's rules (published in his *De re diplomatica*) for distinguishing forgeries, including scrutiny of their script, style, seals, signatures, testimonials, and other intrinsic and extrinsic factors, using an acquired 'taste' derived from long experience, and consulting the views of other document scholars. These previously unavailable and secret documents are research tools of the first order.

Argument swung backwards and forwards about the continuing influence of the Norman Conquest on replacing an old English common-law tradition with one of contracts concerning tenure, serfdom, military duties, and primogeniture, thus producing unequal divisions in society. Douglas says,

> Almost all the controversies of that disputatious age were adorned and disfigured by tales of the Norman Conquest.

Various stories of the Conquest, suitably enhanced with Whiggish nationalistic interpretations, were made available to the public. Butterfield described this process as:

'the tendency in many historians to write on the side of Protestants and Whigs, to praise revolutions provided they have been successful, to emphasise certain principles of progress in the past and to produce a story which is the ratification if not the glorification of the present.'

The resulting nationalistic 'fug' makes viewing the early historiography difficult even today, as there has been endless repetition of the obfuscation, by those with nationalistic views and by historical novelists.

Was the Norman Conquest truly such a national disaster and humiliation? The Whigs thought so ...

The Victorians: 1837–1901

Following the Industrial Revolution, social and revolutionary changes in Europe, developments of nationalism and the introduction of Marxist and other philosophies, there was a transformation in historical thought. The Anglo-Saxon English were proposed to be fighters for social freedoms against the tyranny of Norman 'feudalism', and history is mingled with fiction in heroic literature such as Walter Scott's *Ivanhoe*.[7] Such distortions were convenient for politicians interested in social change. This fed into assertive Victorian mythologies which idealised the Middle Ages and perceived strong Saxon roots.

More people became involved in education. Universities started history courses, libraries were set up, learned societies were founded for the promotion of all sorts of ideas, good or crackpot, and local history societies flourished, although sadly Battle's society was not set up until 1951.

In Victorian academic studies of the Norman Conquest the Anglo-Saxons had a head start. Edward Freeman, who saw English history as a story of the triumphant emergence of the English nation with a free parliament, wrote his huge *History of the Norman Conquest in England* in five volumes (Fig.42) plus an index volume published 1867–79. Within an erudite work of great detail, he rather over glorified Earl Godwin and Harold Godwinson as champions of English nationalism, and his relative lack of critical questioning and degrees of exaggeration left him open to attack. He duly was attacked, and ferociously so, by John Round. In the end, the bitter dispute between Freeman and Round led to some polarisation of historians into pro-Anglo-Saxon and pro-Norman camps which were to continue to distort some writings into the 20th century.

Fortunately, new and closer collaborations with American, French and other international historians helped balance things up at the end of the 19th century. A Danish work by Johannes Steenstrup, *Normannerne*, published concurrently with Freeman's works, started a reassessment of the Scandinavian contribution to English history. Unfortunately, but horribly predictably, this was initially rudely

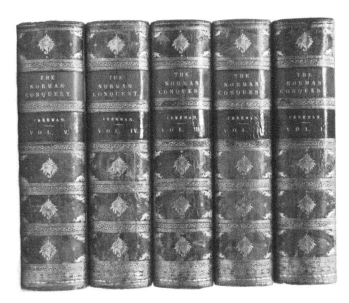

Figure 42. Examples of Freeman's five-volume tome, there is also an Index volume

and xenophobically dubbed in some British historical circles as 'lubrications in an unknown tongue'. But Frank Stenton (1880–1967) fortunately started to bring Scandinavian studies into play, commencing work on his *Danelaw Charters* and *Danes in England* (both studies related to preludes of the Norman invasion) as well as his fine place names studies. By 1908 he would publish his *William the Conqueror*.

Round would point out clearly that the major change in England after the Conquest was in the retention of a king-centric 'curia', with a new, carefully chosen (by the king of course) Norman advisory circle of able and supportive relatives, trusted friends and churchmen, but still without real power (i.e. in no way an elected body and neither de facto replacing the Witan, which was a body with a rather more fluid membership less under the control of the king). Of great importance had been the contracts made under oath that William made with his chief tenants to provide military service in return for baronies, and in turn those contracts that they made locally with their knights, the latter in a rather flexible way – it did not matter how the dues and service were provided as long as they were – and the county sheriff was there to make sure of it. This gave the king a powerful and loyal military machine. This analysis had been advanced two centuries before by Henry Spelman and Robert Cotton but had been ignored and obscured by entrenched misconceptions and the dreaded Whiggish 'fug'.

Early 20th century: 1901–1946

In the 20th century historical writing became more professional and objective and tried to avoid any influence from contemporary events. New approaches challenged historians to rethink interpretations of the past.

The American researcher Charles Haskins (Fig. 43) focused on Normandy (for example see his *The Normans in European History*) and his work gleaned from many French archives highlighted the structure and obligations which had evolved in

Figure 43.
Charles H Haskins
http://en.wikipedia.org/wiki/
Image:Charles.h.haskins.jpg Public Domain

pre-Conquest Normandy, particularly under Duke William II, to be later imposed on post-Conquest England. These were reviewed by François Neveux and David Douglas took up this work and expanded it. Frank Stenton augmented this further, contributing new work on Anglo-Saxon and Scandinavian influences.

Thus, the Conquest started to be placed in a wider European, less English nationalistic context. Increasingly economic, anthropological, historical-geographic, social, and archaeological studies were taken into account.

Late 20th century: 1946–1999

Later 20th century studies challenged further concepts of 'feudalism' and its imposition – or not. It was suggested that systematic change could not have happened immediately post-Conquest but did not deny that lordship and tenure did not exist, as described above.

It was recognized that the Normans in England were essentially pragmatic. Lordship was only one of the bonds of the new society even when associated with land, as there were also ducal, royal, and abbatial rights to consider and sometimes a tenant held lands of more than one lord. Homage was a two way and sometimes multilayered affair with oath taking both to serve and protect. No uniform system of military service existed at first; it was being worked out as there were also paid troops and mercenaries to consider.

Clearly after the Conquest there had been mass land loss and disenfranchisement of the ruling English class. This started with allocation of the royal lands and the very extensive lands previously held by members of the Godwin family, which were the first to be distributed to new Norman lords, if not retained in royal hands.

Elsewhere, most but not all English were 'demoted' to hold parts of their previous lands from a new Norman land holder, but it is more difficult to know what happened to the middle and low-ranking English. A small attempt to illustrate the fate of the English in the local area of eastern Sussex has been made in Foord's *BC to 1066*.

Apart from having a new lord, did life change much at all for ordinary folk if they avoided getting involved in any rebellions? We do know that the Normans essentially abolished slavery.

Robin Fleming examined hundreds of references to proceedings about property rights in *Domesday Book and the Law* and concluded that, if these were not held at baronial level and judged in baronial courts, then some of the disruption had been mitigated by the retention of older pre-Conquest customs at the local level with 'hundred' and 'shire' courts, where about half the jurors were English. Henry II codified the laws after 1154, with 1189 defined as the end of 'time immemorial' and the start of the common law of England, as later interpreted by courts.

The baronial courts became much weakened and permanent professional courts at Westminster and in the shires were established. Thus, was recognised the true start of the creation of a new post-Conquest English common law.

The views of French historians, such as François Neveux, have also become more widely available and we also have a view from the Channel Islander John Le Patourel in his book *The Norman Empire*.

The 2nd Millennium: 2000 onwards

At the opening of the 21st century, studies of the death of Harold and the Norman Conquest and its consequences continue to fascinate historians and others, and the study of its history is thriving, with popular and more or less serious magazines, podcasts and television series, which are usually well edited to remove bloomers and old wives tales, although some veer to the sub-sensational.

Much has appeared on the internet, including BDHS' own series of papers in their *Collectanea* series on the society website. Unfortunately, there is much misleading and sometimes preposterous information on the internet, with admixtures of fact and fiction. Fortunately, there are there are some very excellent recent works available. Of note are: *A Companion to the Anglo-Norman World*, with multiple authors and edited by Harper-Bill and van Houts which was published in 2002 containing overviews of Norman secular and religious administration, and a study of 'feudalism' and lordship; David Bates published his book, based on borrowings from social and political sciences, *The Normans and Empire* in 2013 (Fig.44) offering a new cross-disciplinary interpretive framework for the same period (1066–1204).

A synopsis of a course of seminars at Kings College London said;

> seminars will address the impact of the Norman Conquest on different aspects of government and society, such as land tenure and lordship, military matters, secular and religious architecture, kingship, queenship, government, law, the church, the economy, the formation of national identity, and on different social groups such as the aristocracy, women and the peasantry. The sheer range of engaging subject matter is one reason to opting for this module. There are several others: the profusion and

richness of the sources; the quality of the historiography; the continuing relevance and resonance of this material.

The Battle Conference on Anglo-Norman Studies founded by R. Allen Brown in 1978 continues to attract academics from all over the world (initially it met at Battle, but sadly it is now seldom held in Battle itself) and is an academic annual conference devoted to English and Norman mediaeval history and culture. It focuses primarily, but not exclusively, on the eleventh and twelfth centuries. Its purpose is;

> 'to discuss and forward knowledge on all aspects of Anglo-Norman history, with particular reference to the Anglo-Norman realm, but also to be concerned with the Old English and Scandinavian contribution

Figure 44. *The Normans and Empire* **book cover** Photo: Keith Foord

to the Anglo-Norman achievement in Italy, Sicily, Spain and the Crusades.'

Effects today:

So, what are the lasting effects of Harold's loss and the subsequent Norman Conquest today?

On the local scale '1066 Country' now welcomes non-belligerent visitors from all over the world to see the battlefield and abbey at Battle, the remains of the Roman and Norman castles at Pevensey, the remains of Hastings castle, the surrounding beautiful countryside and coast, as well as later historic structures at Bodiam, Rye, Winchelsea and Bayham. There is a '1066 Country Walk' and 'The 1066 Malfosse Walk' at Battle – a guide to the latter (with history of course!) is available from BDHS as a small book authored by Clephane-Cameron.[8]

The whole country is scattered with old abbeys, priories, castles, churches and cathedrals of post Norman origin each with its own rich history, making it a paradise for a history loving tourist.

Britain has different legal systems from most of Europe, based on precedent stretching back centuries – exported to the Commonwealth, Ireland, and the USA, where time has created variations and even more and different precedents.

The word-rich English language with its many incorporated Scandinavian and 10,000 Norman French words is now spoken across the world. We now arguably have more shared historical ties with western continental Europe than Scandinavia; we might have remained closer to the Scandinavian sphere if Harold had not lost.

Without doubt, Harold's defeat and the Norman Conquest had a huge impact on England. The invasion did not immediately change the face of English society except at the very top, but as England further developed under the Normans their actions would change English culture, with the impact still found with mainly social and anachronistic consequences in Britain today. For example, students with 'Norman' surnames remain over-represented at Oxford and Cambridge Universities. William's 'Harrying of the North' may to a small extent help to explain the persisting relative deprivation of the north that still gives modern Britain Europe's highest regional inequality.

For illustration the maps (figures 45 and 46) show respectively the regional differences in family wealth and income per head in England, Scotland and Wales in 2015. Much, but not all, of the wealth differences are due to property values. The data on which these maps are based came from the UK Office of National Statistics.

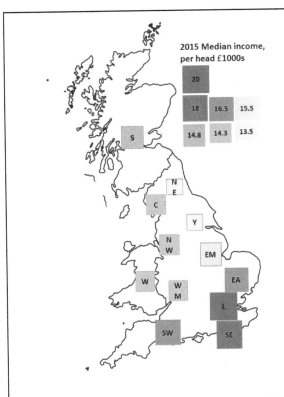

Much of the country remains the property of a few elite families and corporations. According to Cahill[9] in 2002, 0.3% of the population owned two thirds of the country and descendants of Normans as a broad group remained wealthier than the general population. Shrubsole[10] found a not dissimilar picture in 2019.

There is a fascination with history, with both fictional and non-fictional TV and streamed history programmes and fictionally distorted films.

Figure 45.

Figure 46

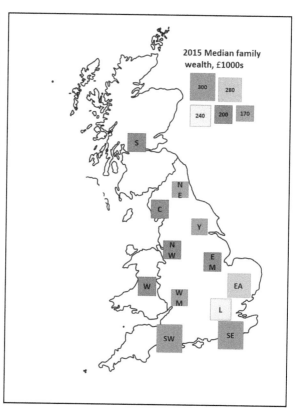

2015 Median family wealth, £1000s

Recently historians have stressed post-Conquest sociological continuity of the middle and lower groups of English society, questioning whether the invasion should be viewed as a cataclysm or a catalyst for change. Douglas clearly thought that the Conquest had significantly affected the evolution of the average Briton's way of life and customs, but that the very awareness of that had tended to blur appreciation of the qualities of the prior Anglo-Scandinavian society that existed before 1066 and actually persisted at a local level after 1066, in parallel with changes 'at the top'. But we should remember that Anglo-Saxon slavery was abolished post Conquest.

The Norman world which was a harsher militaristic and more materialistic world had lagged marginally in arts and literature, which the Anglo-Saxon and Celtic worlds had embraced more fully. But Normandy was, in terms of church structure, architecture and arguably theology generally more advanced, although more obedient to Rome, which was probably the main reason why Pope Alexander II is said to have given William's adventure his blessing.

Much of the lower levels of administration after the Conquest were still based on English norms, but the Norman elites introduced a new overarching executive administration, reinvigorated the religious world and were economically, politically, and militarily ruthless masters of all they held.

What is certain is that in the 21st century any new historical concepts and ideas now need to be soundly evidence based, critically assessed and to avoid modern political or social bias and particularly false truths. The era of introverted, xenophobic, and controversial Anglo-centric scholarship is hopefully over. No longer should we contemplate the Conquest in terms of modern nationalism, Whig theories, Protestant fervour or nineteen-century liberalism or even the 21st century plague of fake news.

British nationalism has its own unique balanced history, warts and all, quite a few lows and many triumphs, but it would have been different if Harold had won – still unique, just in an unknowable way, for we do not know what would have happened during and after his reign if he had survived 'Hastings'.

Notes

1   Besmier, R. *La Coutume de Normandie, Histoire externe* (1935).

2   Neveux, F. 'Le contexte historique de la rédaction des coutumiers normands' *Annales de Normandie* 61 (2011x2).

3   There may be some doubt about this being given and the story being invented later, perhaps by William of Poitiers after the event. The papal banner is represented several times in the BT.

4   Yeatman, RJ. and Sellar, WC. *1066 and All That: A Memorable History of England* (1930).

5   See Hagger, M. 'The Norman vicomte, c1035–1135: What did he do?' in: *Anglo-Norman Studies*, Vol. 29, (2007).

6   During this period Sir Robert Bruce Cotton died, with the collection passing to his son.

7   Published just before Victoria came to the throne, but it set the scene.

8   Clephane-Cameron, N. *The Malfosse Walk* (2nd Edition, 2020).

9   Cahill, K. *Who owns Britain and Ireland* (2002).

10   Shrubsole, G. *Who owns England?* (2019).

History could not be regarded as a nearly dispassionate
science until after the dawn of the 20th century.
It still cannot be regarded as totally dispassionate
in the 21st century, as there are always interpretive
disagreements over matters on which there can never be
agreement, as the evidence is inadequate.
These arouse unwarranted passion...

The era of introverted, xenophobic, and controversial
Anglocentric scholarship is hopefully over.

Selected Bibliographies

Part 1

Abels, R. 'English Logistics and military administration, 871–1066: The Impact of the Viking Wars', in *Jorgensen AN and Clausen, BL (Eds): Papers from an international research seminar at the Danish National Museum, Copenhagen, 2–4 May 1996: Military aspects of Scandinavian society in a European perspective, AD1–1300,* (1997)

Anonymous. *Vita Edwardi Regis* British Library Harley MS 526 (for a translation see Luard below)

Anscombe, A. 'The Pedigree of Godwine' *Transactions of the Royal Historical Society,* 37, (1913): 129–50

Arnold, N. 'The Defeat of the sons of Harold in 1069' *Battalia* Vol.1 (2017) ISSN 2516-0451

Ashe, L and Ward, EJ. *Conquests in Eleventh Century England: 1016, 1066* (2020)

Barlow, F. *Edward the Confessor,* (1997)

Barlow, F (Ed.) *The 'Carmen de Hastingae Proelio' of Guy Bishop of Amiens.* (1999)

Barlow, F. *The Godwins: The Rise and Fall of a Noble Dynasty,* (2002)

Barlow, LW. The Antecedents of Earl Godwine of Wessex', *New England Historical and Genealogical Register,* lxi, (1957)

Barral i Altet, X. and Bates, D. *La Tapisserie de Bayeux,* (2019)

Bates, D and Curry, A (Eds*.) England and Normandy in the Middle Ages* (1995)

Bates, D. *Bishop Remigius of Lincoln, 1067-92* (1992)

Bates, D. (Ed.) *1066 in Perspective,* (2018)

Bates, D. *The Normans and Empire* (2013)

Bates, D. *Normandy Before 1066,* (1982)

Bates, D. *William the Conqueror,* (2016)

Baxter, S. Edward the Confessor and the Succession Question', in Mortimer, R (Ed.), *Edward the Confessor: The Man & the Legend,* (2009)

Baxter, S. *The Earls of Mercia – Lordship and Power in late Anglo-Saxon England* (2007)

Beattie, W. 'Waltham Abbey' in *The Castles and Abbeys of England, Vol. 1* (1842) (available as a Project Gutenberg e-book)

Beech, G. 'England and Aquitaine in the century before the Norman Conquest' *Anglo-Saxon England* 19 (1990)

Beltz, GF. ' Observations on the Coffin-Plate and History of Gunilda, sister of the Saxon King Harold II' in a Letter to Sir Henry Ellis, *Archaeologia, 25*, 398-410 (1832)

Bernstein, D. 'The Blinding of Harold and the Meaning of the Bayeux Tapestry' *Anglo-Norman Studies* V (1982)

Bernstein, D. *The Mystery of the Bayeux Tapestry* (1986)

Besmier, R. *La Coutume de Normandie, Histoire externe* (1935)

Bloch, RH. 'Animal Fables, the Bayeux Tapestry and the making of the Anglo-Norman

World', *Poetica,* vol. 37, no. 3/4, (2005)

Bolton, T. *The Empire of Cnut the Great: Conquest and the Consolidation of Power in Northern Europe in the Early Eleventh Century.* (2009)

Bosanquet, G. (Trans.) *Eadmer's History of Recent Events in England: 'Historia Novorum in Anglia'',* (1964)

Boyle, JR. 'Who was Eddeva?' *Transactions of the East Riding Antiquarian Society* 4 (1896)

Brady, R. *A Complete History of England* (1685)

Brown, R. Allen. *The Norman Conquest of England– Sources and Documents* (1995)

Bruce, JC. *The Bayeux Tapestry Elucidated* (1856)

Butterfield, H. *The Whig interpretation of History* (1931)

Chefneux, H. 'Les fables dans la tapisserie de Bayeux', *Romania* Vol. LX (1934): 1–35

Clarke, P. *The English Nobility under Edward the Confessor* (1994)

Clephane-Cameron, N. *The Malfosse Walk* (2nd Edition, 2020)

Clephane-Cameron, N. Various personal communications and extracts from Foord, K. and Clephane-Cameron, N. *1066 and the Battle of Hastings, Preludes, Events and Postscripts.* (2021)

Cowdrey, HEJ. 'Towards an Interpretation of the Bayeux Tapestry', *Anglo-Norman Studies*, X , (1987)

Crouch, D. *The Normans: The History of a Dynasty,* 2006,

Curry, A. and Foard, G. 'Where are the dead of medieval battles? A preliminary survey' *Journal of Conflict Archaeology* 11, 2-3 (2016)

Darlington, RR. (Ed.), P. McGurk (Ed. & Trans.), Bray J. (Trans.). *The Chronicle of John of Worcester: Volume II: The Annals from 450–1066,* (1995)

Davis, RHC. *The Normans and their Myth* (1976)

d'Eyncourt, CT. 'Memoir of the Leaden Plate, the Memorial of William d'Eyncourt, preserved in the Cathedral Library at Lincoln' in *Memoirs illustrative of the History and Antiquities of the County and City of Lincoln* at the AGM of the Archaeological Institute of Great Britain and Ireland– 1848 (1850)

DeVries, K. 'Harold Godwinson in Wales: Military Legitimacy in late Anglo-Saxon England' in Abels, RP. and Bachrach, BS. (Eds.) *The Normans and their Adversaries at War – Essays in Memory of C. Warren Hollister* (2001)

Dennis, C. 'The strange death of King Harold II' *The Historian* (Spring 2009)

Douglas, DC. and Greenaway GW. (Eds.) *English Historical Documents 1042-1189* (1968)

Douglas, DC. 'The Norman Conquest and British historians' *13th lecture on the David Murray Foundation in the University of Glasgow delivered on February 20th, 1946 (1946)*

Douglas, DC. *William the Conqueror – The Norman Impact upon England* (1964)

Dugdale, W, *Baronage of England* (1675)

Dunlop, J. 'The Story of the Rye road – Some Thoughts on Harold's Route' *BDHS Transactions* (1962-3)

English Heritage and Essex County Council. *Extensive Urban Survey– Essex: Historic Towns Assessment Report Waltham Abbey* (1999)

Fell, C. 'The Icelandic saga of Edward the Confessor: its version of the Anglo-Saxon emigration to Byzantium' *Published online by Cambridge University Press: 26 September 2008*

Fellows-Jensen, G. 'The Myth of Harold II's survival in the Scandinavian Sagas' in Owen-Crocker, GR. (Ed.). *King Harold II and the Bayeux Tapestry* (2005)

Fletcher, R. *Bloodfeud – Murder and Revenge in Anglo-Saxon England* (2002)

Foord, K. *BC to 1066* (2020)

Foord, K. *Conquest to Dissolution 1067-1538* (2019)

Foord, K. 'R4.2a A Critique and Comparison of "Companion Rolls of the Conquest", some known as 'Battle Abbey Rolls' *via BDHS website*

Foord, K. 'R4.2b Data underlying the "Companion Rolls of the Conquest" – paper R4.2a': *via BDHS website*

Foord, K. and Clephane-Cameron, N. *1066 and the Battle of Hastings, Preludes, Events and Postscripts.* (2021)

Foys, M., Terkla, D. and Overbey, K (Eds.) *The Bayeux Tapestry: New Interpretations* (2009)

Freeman, EA. *The History of the Norman Conquest of England* (6 Vols. 1867-79)

Gade, KE. 'Northern Light on the Battle of Hastings', *Viator,* Vol 28, (1997): 65

Gameson, R. (Ed.) *The study of the Bayeux Tapestry* (1997)

Gardon, F. *Histoire de l'abbeye de la Chaise-Dieu* (17th century, published 1912). *Available On-line at BnF*

Gaussin, P-R. *L'Abbaye de la Chaise-Dieu (1043-1518)– L'abbaye en Auvergne et son rayonnement dans la Chrétienté* (1962)

Giles, JA. *William of Malmesbury's Chronicle of the Kings of England,* (1847)

Giles, JA. *Scriptores Rerum Gestarum Williemi Conquestoris in Unum Collecti* (1845) This contains various less well-known documents in Latin, Norman-French and even one in Old English related to William. It includes the *Carmen* in the original Latin

Gilliat-Smith, E. *The Story of Bruges* (1909)

Gillingham, JB. *Conquests, Catastrophe and Recovery* (2014)

Gillingham, JB. '1066 and warfare: the context and place (Senlac) of the Battle of Hastings' in Bates, D. (Ed.) *1066 in Perspective,* (2018)

Gillingham, JB. ''Up with Orthodoxy' – In Defence of Vegetian Warfare' *Journal of Medieval Military History* Vol.2 (2004)

Greene, C. *The Battle Tapestry – A Visual History of the Town of Battle 1066-1115* (2019)

Grierson, P. 'A Visit of Earl Harold to Flanders in 1056', *The English Historical Review,* Vol. 51, No. 201, (1936): 90–97

Hariulf, M. (Lot, F. Ed.). *Chronique de Saint-Riquier,* (1894/2010)

Harper-Bill, C. and van Houts EMC. (Eds.) *A Companion to the Anglo-Norman World* (2002)

Haskins, CH. *The Normans in European History* (1916)

Hicks, C. *The Bayeux Tapestry: The Life Story of a Masterpiece* (2007)

Hooper, N. 'The Housecarls in England in the Eleventh Century.' in Strickland, M. (Ed.), *Anglo-Norman Warfare, (1992)*

Howard ,I. 'Harold II: A Throne-worthy King' in Owen-Crocker, GR. (Ed.) *King Harold II and the Bayeux Tapestry* (2005)

Howarth, D. *1066: The Year of the Conquest,* 1983

Hudson, B. 'The Family of Harold Godwinson and the Irish Sea Province' *Journal of the Royal Society.of Antiquaries of Ireland* Vol. 109, 92-100 (1979)

Huggins, PJ., Bascombe, KN. and Huggins, RM. Excavations of the Collegiate and Augustinian Churches, Waltham Abbey, Essex, 1984–87, *Archaeological Journal,* 146:1 (1989)

Huggins, PJ., Bascombe, KN. and Huggins, RM. 'Excavations at Waltham Abbey, Essex, 1985–1991: Three Pre-Conquest Churches and Norman Evidence', *Archaeological*

Journal, 149:1, (1992)

Jones, C. 'The Literary sources for the 1066 Battle of Fulford' *via https://www.academia. edu*

Jones, C. *The Yorkshire Preface to the Bayeux Tapestry* (2005)

Jones, T. *The Chronicle of the Princes* (1955)

Knowles, Dom D., Brooke, CNL. and London, V. *The Heads of Religious Houses: England and Wales 940-1216* (1972)

Keats-Rohan, K. 'Domesday People revisited' *Foundations*, 4 (2012)

Laporte, J. 'Les opérations navales en Manche et Mer du Nord pendant l'année 1066'. *Annales de Normandie. 17ᵉ année No.1* (1967)

Larson, LM. *Canute the Great*, (1912)

Larson, LM. *The King's Household in England before the Norman Conquest*, (1904)

Lawson, MK. *Cnut – England's Viking King 1016–1035*, (2011)

Le Patourel, J. *The Norman Empire* (1976)

Lemagnen, S. *La Tapisserie de Bayeux. Une découverte pas à pas : A Step-by-Step Discovery* (2015)

Lemagnen, S. *The Bayeux Tapestry* (2019)

Lemmon, CH. *The Field of Hastings* (1977)

Lewis, M. 'Myths and Mysteries of the Bayeux Tapestry' in Bates, D (Ed.) *1066 in Perspective* (2018)

Lewis, MJ., Owen-Crocker, GR and Terkla, D. *The Bayeux Tapestry: New Approaches* (2011)

Licence, T. 'Edward the Confessor and the Succession Question: A Fresh Look at the Sources', *Anglo-Norman Studies 39: 2016* (2017)

Licence, T. *Edward the Confessor – Last of the Royal Blood*, (2020)

Longnon, A. *Pouillés de la province de Rouen* (1903) On-line at BnF

Loyd, LC., Clay, CT. and Douglas, DC. (Eds.) *The Origins of Some Anglo-Norman Families* (1951 reprinted 1975)

Luard, HR. (Ed.) *Lives of Edward the Confessor*,(1858)

Pálsson, H. and Magnusson, M. (Eds. and Trans.) *King Harald's Saga– Harald Hardradi of Norway:* From Snorri Sturluson's *Heimskringla* (1976)

Mason, E. *The House of Godwine – The History of a Dynasty*, (2004)

Matthews, S. 'The Content and Construction of the Vita Haraldi' in Owen-Crocker, GR. (Ed.) *King Harold II and the Bayeux Tapestry* (2005)

Montfaucon, Abbé B. de, *Les Monumens de la Monarchie Françoise* Vol. 2 *(1730)*

Morillo, S. (Ed.) *The Battle of Hastings*, (1996): 3–53

Morris, M. *The Anglo-Saxons – A History of the Beginnings of England* (2021)

Morris, M. *The Norman Conquest* (2013)

Mortimer, R. (Ed.), *Edward the Confessor: The Man & the Legend*, (2009)

Morton C. and Muntz, H. (Trans. and Eds.) *The Carmen de Hastingae Proelio of Bishop Guy of Amiens* (1972)

Musgrove, D. and Lewis, M. *The Story of the Bayeux Tapestry* (2021)

Naismith, R. 'England before 1066' in Bates, D. (Ed.) *1066 in Perspective*, (2018)

Nelson, JL. et al (Authors and Eds.) *PASE – Prosopography of Anglo-Saxon England.* https://pase.ac.uk/index.html

Neveux, F. 'Le contexte historique de la rédaction des coutumiers normands' *Annales de Normandie* 61 (2011/2)

Neveux, F. *La Normandie des ducs aux rois, Xe-XIIe siècle* (1998)

Neveux, F. *The Normans* (2006)

O'Brian, H. *Queen Emma and the Vikings,* (2005)

Otter, M. 'Baudri of Borgeuil, 'to Countess Adela'' *The Journal of Medieval Latin* Vol. 11 (2001)

Owen-Crocker, GR. (Ed.) King Harold II and the Bayeux Tapestry (2005)

Pastan, EC. 'Montfaucon as Reader of the Bayeux Tapestry' in Marquartdt, JT. and Jordan, A. (Eds.) *Medieval Art and Architecture after the Middle Ages* (2009)

Planché, JR *The Conqueror and his Companions: Vol 2* (1874)

Pye, DW. 'The Magnus Inscription' *Sussex Notes and Queries 16* (November, 1965)

Rex, P. *Harold II. The Doomed Saxon King* (2005)

Roach, L. *Kingship and Consent in Anglo-Saxon England 871-978 – Assemblies and the State in the early Middle Ages* (2013)

Rowley, T. *An Archaeological Study of the Bayeux Tapestry* (2016

Searle, E. (Ed. and Trans.) *'The Chronicle of Battle Abbey'* (1980)

Sharpe, R. 'King Harold's Daughter' in North, W. and Morillo, S. (Ed.) *Haskins Society Journal XIX – Studies in Medieval History* (2008 for 2007)

Shepard, J. The English and Byzantium: A Study of their role in the Byzantine Army in the later Eleventh Century. *Traditio* ((1973), *29,* 53-92.

Skarbek-Kozietulski, M. 'More about Magnus, Count of Wroclaw' *Genealogia Mediaevalis Genetica, (2011) via https://www.academia.edu*

Stafford, P. *Queen Emma and Queen Edith: Queenship and Women's Power in Eleventh Century England* (2001)

Stothard, CA. 'Some Observations on the Bayeux Tapestry', *Archaeologia* 19 (1821) copied in Gameson, R. (Ed.) *The study of the Bayeux Tapestry* (1997)

Swanton, M. (Trans. and Ed.) *The Anglo-Saxon Chronicle,* (2000)

Taylor, A. 'Belrem' in Chibnall, M. (Ed.) *Anglo-Norman Studies,* XIV, (1991): 1–23

Thompson, K. 'Being the Ducal Sister: The Role of Adelaide of Aumale' in Crouch, D. and Thomson, K. (Eds.) *Normandy and its Neighbours 900-1250; Essays for David Bates* (2011)

Thorpe, L. *The Bayeux Tapestry and the Norman Invasion*, 1973

Thomas, HM. *The English and The Normans: Ethnic Hostility, Assimilation, and Identity 1066– c. 1220 (2002)*

Walker, I. *Harold the Last Anglo-Saxon King*, (2000)

Ward, EJ. 'Child Kings and the Norman Conquest: representations of Association and Succession' in Ashe,L and Ward EJ. *Conquests in Eleventh Century England: 1016, 1066* (2020)

Watkiss, I. and Chibnal, M. (Eds. and Trans.) *The Waltham Chronicle* (1992)

Weir, A. *Britain's Royal Families – The Complete Genealogy* (2008)

Williams, A. and Martin, GH. (Eds.) *Domesday Book*(1992)

Williams, A. '1066 and the English' in Bates, D. (Ed.) *1066 in Perspective,* (2018)

Williams, A. *The English and the Norman Conquest* (1995)

    Williams, A. 'Some notes and considerations on problems connected with the English royal succession, 860-1066' in *Proceedings of the Battle Conference 1978*, Eds. R Allen Brown and M Chibnall (1979)

Williams, A and Martin, GH (Eds.) *Domesday Book – A Complete Translation* (2002)

Williams, G. 'Was the last Anglo-Saxon King of England a Queen? A possible posthumous Coinage of Harold II' *The Yorkshire Numismatist* IV (2012)

Wilson, DM. *'The Bayeux Tapestry'* (1985)

Winters, W. 'Passages in the Life and Reign of Harold, the last of the Saxon Kings'. *Transactions of the Royal Historical Society* Vol.5 (1877)

Zajac, NAM. *Women Between West and East: the Inter-Rite Marriages of the Kyivan Rus' Dynasty, ca. 1000-1204*. PhD Thesis, Centre for Medieval Studies, University of Toronto (2017)

Web based bibliography for Part 1
(as at October, 2021)

https://aclerkofoxford.blogspot.com/2014/10/hastings-and-hermit-king.html

https://www.bayeuxmuseum.com/la-tapisserie-de-bayeux/decouvrir-la-tapisserie-de-bayeux/explorer-la-tapisserie-de-bayeux-en-ligne/

https://www.caitlingreen.org/2015/05/medieval-new-england-black-sea.html

https://chesterwalls.info/stjohn.html

https://commons.wikimedia.org/wiki/Category:Stothard_engravings_of_the_Bayeux_tapestry_1823

https://historicalmenandwomen.blogspot.com/2019/11/king-harold-at-chester.html

https://opendomesday.org/

https://pase.ac.uk/jsp/index.jsp

https://domesday.pase.ac.uk/

https://epns.nottingham.ac.uk/

https://silo.tips/download/contents-preface-bibliography-108-index-116#modals

http://www.vsnrweb-publications.org.uk/Hemings%20thattr.pdf

http://www.walthamabbeychurch.co.uk/history.htm

https://zamekczersk.pl/en/history_1109

Part 2

Bates, D. 'Normandy and England after 1066' *English Historical Review*, CCCCXIII (Oct 1989)

Cahill, K. *Who owns Britain and Ireland* (2002)

Chibnall, M. *The Debate on the Norman Conquest* (1999)

Clephane-Cameron, N. *The 1066 Malfosse Walk* (2020)

Davis, RHC. *The Normans and their Myth* (1976)

Douglas, DC. 'The Norman Conquest and British historians' *13th lecture on the David Murray Foundation in the University of Glasgow delivered on February 20th, 1946* (1946)

Fleming, R. *Domesday Book and the Law* (1998)

Foord, K. 'The Rapes of Sussex, Hundreds of Hastings Rape and the people of the Rape of Hastings to 1538' (2018) *via BDHS website*

Hale, M. *The History of the Common Law in England* (published posthumously in 1713)

Harper-Bill, C and van Houts EMC (Eds.) *A Companion to the Anglo-Norman World* (2002)

Mabillon, J. *De re Diplomatica* (1681)

Madox, T. *Formulare Anglicanum* (1702)

Rymer , T. *The Foedera* (1642x3-1713)
Shrubsole, G. *Who owns England?* (2019)
Stenton, DM (Ed.) *Preparatory to Anglo-Saxon England: Being the Collected Papers of Frank Merry Stenton* (1970)
Stenton, F. *Anglo-Saxon England* (1943, 3rd Edition 1971)

Web based bibliography for Part 2
(as at October, 2021)

https://en.wikipedia.org/wiki/Robert_Brady_(writer)
https://en.wikipedia.org/wiki/Jean_Mabillon
https://en.wikipedia.org/wiki/Thomas_Madox
http://www.historyofparliamentonline.org/volume/1509-1558/member/rastell-john-1468-1536
https://www.parliament.uk/about/living-heritage/evolutionofparliament/originsofparliament/birthofparliament/keydates/1215to1399/
https://www.parliament.uk/about/living-heritage/evolutionofparliament/originsofparliament/birthofparliament/keydates/1399to1603/

BDHS has no responsibility for the continuity or accuracy of URLs for external or third-party websites, nor for the present or continuing accuracy or appropriateness of those websites referred to in this publication

Books published by
Battle and District Historical Society

George Kiloh, *English Rural Revolution 1830–1870* (to be published in 2022)
Geoge Kiloh, *Battle Characters through the Ages*, 2021
Neil Clephane-Cameron, *1066 Malfosse Walk*, 2nd edition 2020
George Kiloh, *The Brave Remembered,* 2015

These three books make up the 'Battle Trilogy': a history of eastern Sussex from pre-history to the Dissolution of the Monasteries via the Battle of Hastings ... BC to 1538:
Keith Foord & Neil Clephane-Cameron, *1066 and the Battle of Hastings,* 2nd edition 2021
Keith Foord, *Conquest to Dissolution 1067–1538*, 2019
Keith Foord, *BC to 1066*, 2020

Available to purchase from Battle and District Historical Society,
https://battlehistorysociety.com

Other history books published by members of BDHS

Christina Greene, *The Battle Tapestry*, 2019***
Adrian and Sarah Hall, Editors, *Battle at War 1939–45*, 2019**
Keith Foord, *The Methodist Road to Battle*, 2013*
Keith Foord, *Winchelsea Methodist Chapel,* 2013*
Keith Foord, *Battle Abbey and Battle Churches since 1066*, 2011*

*Available from Battle Methodist Church, Emmanuel Centre,
Harrier Lane, Battle TN33 0FL
battlemethodistchurch@btconnect.com   https://bmc.chessck.co.uk

** Available from Battle Museum of Local History, The Almonry,
High Street, Battle TN33 0EA
enquiries@battlemuseum.com   https//www.battlelocalhistory.com

*** Available from tina@greene.org.uk

All the above books should be available from all good booksellers, although maybe only to special order and with short delays.

Index

Page numbers in *italics* refer to information in figures and charts